THEY DON'T WASH THEIR SOCKS!

KATHLYN GAY is the author of more than 50 books. She is a mother and grandmother who obviously likes sports. She lives in Elkart, Indiana, with her husband.

THEY DON'T WASH THEIR SOCKS!
SPORTS SUPERSTITIONS

Kathlyn Gay

Illustrated by
John Kerschbaum

AN AVON CAMELOT BOOK

For Doug, our family's all-around sports trivia expert, with special thanks for help with interviews

AVON BOOKS
A division of
The Hearst Corporation
1350 Avenue of the Americas
New York, New York 10019

Text copyright © 1990 by Kathlyn Gay
Illustrations copyright © 1990 by John Kerschbaum
Front cover design by Georg Brewer
Published by arrangement with Walker and Company
Library of Congress Catalog Card Number: 89-28562
ISBN: 0-380-71302-0
RL: 5.7

The Walker edition contains the following Library of Congress Cataloging in Publication Data:

Gay, Kathlyn.
    They don't wash their socks : sports superstitions / by Kathlyn Gay ; illustrations by John Kerschbaum.
    Includes bibliographical references.
Summary: Examines superstitions held by individuals or teams in all the major sports.
    1. Sports—Folklore—Juvenile literature.   2. Superstition—
Juvenile literature.   [1. Sports—Folklore.   2. Superstition.]
I. Kerschbaum, John, ill.   II. Title.
GR887.G39   1990   398'.355—dc20   89-28562

First Avon Camelot Printing: April 1991

CAMELOT TRADEMARK REG. U.S. PAT. OFF. AND IN OTHER COUNTRIES, MARCA REGISTRADA, HECHO EN U.S.A.

Printed in the U.S.A..

OPM   10   9   8   7   6   5   4   3   2

TABLE OF CONTENTS

★ 1 ★

BASEBALL— THE MOST SUPERSTITIOUS SPORT?

Baseball. It's America's national pastime. But it also has been called the most superstitious sport. Those who play the game or follow baseball hear a lot about how to find good luck or avoid bad luck on the field.

Many stories have circulated about former Chicago White Sox hitter Harold Baines, for example. Baines, who is usually quite talkative, has been called the "silent slugger," because he won't discuss his hits or little else while he's batting well. During the early part of the 1989 season, Baines led the American League in hits, and except for simple yes or no responses refused to talk to reporters or others about his game. To do so, he thought might invite bad luck, breaking his successful streak.

Superstitions have been a part of baseball ever since the game was officially organized. When hay wagons were a common sight it was a good omen if a player passed a wagonload of hay on the way to the ballpark. A load of empty barrels also was a good luck sign.

On the other hand, a player never wanted to see a dog cross the playing field before the first pitch. That was bad luck. And nobody wanted a black cat—long a symbol of misfortune—to cross his path. In fact, sometimes black cats were deliberately used to try to bring bad luck to opponents. Once in Philadelphia, players on the Phillies team carried black cats onto the ball field in an attempt to harass one member of the opposing Brooklyn Dodgers. But Jackie Robinson, the first black man in major-league baseball, ignored the ill will, as he had done many other times when players and fans had tried to put a hex on him. His dramatic plays helped the Dodgers win many games, and he eventually was elected to the Baseball Hall of Fame.

Lucky Mascots from the Past

Early in the history of the game, only males were hired to handle the bats. Batboys often doubled as team mascots, bearers of good luck. It was common practice to touch a batboy or rub his head to ensure a hit.

One unusual mascot in professional baseball was not a batboy, however. He called himself a pitcher and he came to the New York Giants baseball club in 1911, introducing himself as Charles Victor Faust from Kansas. Giants manager John McGraw wondered what this gangly character in his Sunday-best suit and black derby expected to do for the team.

8

"I'm destined to help the Giants win the national league pennant," Faust said.

Such a claim had to be tested. So McGraw asked Faust to take off his coat and hat and show his stuff. As it turned out, Faust was no ballplayer. But McGraw decided not to push his or the team's luck if this strange fellow could have an effect on the team's destiny. So he spread the word among his players. He would try Faust at bat and the team should make sure he got a home run.

Everybody on the field cooperated. On the first pitch, the ball dribbled off Faust's bat toward the shortstop, who fumbled around and managed to throw to first. But Faust was called "safe." With the coach urging him on, Faust went around the bases, sliding with assists into second, third, and then home. Dusting off his Sunday-best, Faust beamed with pride and the team christened him Charles "Victory" Faust.

McGraw decided to take Faust along when the team left for a road trip that night. From then on, Charles "Victory" was part of the Giants' unofficial lineup. He warmed up for every game, but never pitched. Still, he continually reminded everyone that he had been sent to help win the pennant.

Charles "Victory" made a believer out of McGraw when the Giants captured the pennant that season. Faust turned up for the next two seasons and the team continued to win. For three consecutive years the pennant belonged to the Giants. When Charles "Victory" Faust died in 1914, the team's winning streak died, too. The Giants lost the pennant that year.

Pregame Hijinx

Many superstitious practices in baseball take place before the game. A player might put on his uniform in a specific order or eat the same kind of meal every game day. Another might meditate for hours, or go through a warm-up routine that never varies from one pregame period to the next. Keith Hernandez formerly of the New York Mets says he does crossword puzzles for twenty minutes before each game. Former Cubs pitcher Paul Moskau always had to shake hands with the team's public relations director and insisted that the P.R. man wish him good luck before he left the locker room.

Some pregame rituals became quite complex. Cy Young award-winner Steve Stone believed his success was partly due to his breakfast routine. In the early part of one season with the Baltimore Orioles, Stone had breakfast with a sportswriter and after that won a couple of games in a row. From then on, Stone insisted on the same ritual to "keep his luck going." And the sportswriter dutifully appeared for breakfast prior to games in which Stone would pitch. The result? Twenty-five wins and the outstanding pitcher award for Stone that season.

When Mike Norris pitched for the Oakland Athletics, he extended his pregame ritual through midafternoon. His routine included watching TV soap operas and eating soul food for luck. When his team was at bat, Norris would always go to the clubhouse, a ritual he felt prevented any misfortune befalling the A's while on the field. He also tried to wear the same shoes every time he pitched.

Wade Boggs of the Red Sox has become well known for his pregame ritual. It always begins at 2:00 in the afternoon with a chicken dinner. He believes chicken improves his hitting. After his arrival at the clubhouse, his routine is precisely scheduled. He puts on his uniform at 3:30. Then all exercises, from batting practice to final wind sprints, take place at a specific time and exactly on the minute.

Managers and coaches also have their pregame acts. Years ago a Boston Braves manager made sure that all advertisements with the color yellow were removed from the ballpark before the game. Players, too, were checked for any yellow in their clothing. Yellow was considered bad luck for the team, perhaps because the color long has been associated with cowardice.

Changing the lineup may be one way a coach tries to court good luck before a game, especially if his team is in a slump. Former Chicago Cubs coach Ruben Amaro always posted his lineup in a certain place in the dugout. But after a long losing streak, Amaro decided to try to do what he could to change his team's luck. So he posted the lineup sheet on a different dugout wall. That day the Cubs won a doubleheader over the St. Louis Cardinals.

Watch Those Lines and Bases!

"Step on a crack and you'll break your mother's back." Maybe that saying has something to do with the baseball players who take extreme precautions to

11

avoid stepping on the foul line, an act they believe could bring bad luck.

Some players make a ritual of getting safely across the foul line. Several players have developed stylized hops. Others cross the foul line at exactly the same place every time they leave the field at the end of an inning.

A number of players are also superstitious about baselines. One former top major-leaguer, Joe Niekro, never crossed the running lane leading from the batter's box to first base. If at the end of an inning Niekro happened to be near first base, he would not consider taking the shortest route to the dugout. Rather than trot diagonally across the field, he squared off his course, jogging along to the end of the running lane, the only place where he would make his exit, as this diagram shows:

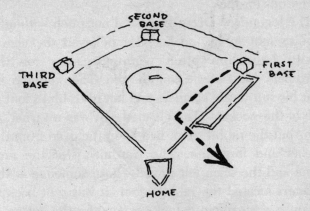

The bases themselves are another good or bad luck item. Former shortstop Larry Bowa used to jump on third base with both feet for luck. Other players feel it's lucky to step on third (or second or first) base before running off the field at the end of an inning.

Collectibles and "Carry-ons"

Finding a penny, players once believed, could bring a hit. But the charm wouldn't work if the coin was "planted" for a batter to find or given to the player by a teammate, fan, or other well-wisher.

Hairpins are another good omen, related to the oft-repeated ditty: "See a pin and pick it up/All the day you'll have good luck/See a pin and let it lie/All the day you'll have to cry." One minor-league player of the past is said to have collected over two hundred hairpins, one for each hit that season. But no ballplayer collected these talismans as avidly as old-time player and manager Leo Durocher. Wherever he went, he looked for all types of hairpins, gathering thousands for luck.

The legendary Dizzy Dean did not pitch without a rabbit's foot in his pocket. He believed the charm would help him pitch winning games for the Cardinals. Most of the time he did. Then one day he sent his suit to the cleaners and left his rabbit's foot in one of the pockets. The cleaned suit was returned to him, but the rabbit's foot had been removed from the pocket and forgotten. The Cardinals lost the next game and the team felt jinxed—until someone at the cleaners located the rabbit's foot. It was sent back to Dean, and his pitching luck changed for the better.

Even today some ballplayers, as well as people in other walks of life, would swear by the charm of the rabbit's foot. The superstition is based on an ancient British belief in the supernatural powers of such animals as the hare (and later the rabbit when hares became scarce), fox, and cat. Carrying a foot or tail of any of these animals was thought to protect the owner.

Players, like fans, collect baseball cards and display them for luck (or to hex an opponent). In their pockets or shoes or under their hats, they carry lucky charms: the familiar four-leaf clover, a polished stone, or even a crumpled-up soft drink cup. Don Mattingly of the Yankees carries a packet of sugar in his back pocket. This practice stems from the time the Yankees general manager suggested that players who were in a slump eat sugar to raise their energy levels. It worked for

Mattingly. In the next game he got two hits, so the sugar packet has become a good luck charm for him. Players also keep good luck items in their lockers—photos, stuffed animals, and even frilly women's underwear.

Magic in Pitching

Pitchers seem to get involved in more rituals than any other players in baseball. There is a long-standing superstition that a team can be jinxed if anyone mentions that the pitcher has a no-hitter going. Announcing a no-hitter or perfect game before it has been accomplished is tempting Fate—the very next pitch might favor the opposing team.

When a pitcher is on a losing streak, he may look for something to change his luck. Houston Astros pitcher Jim Deshaies was really upset when his team lost eleven games in a row. He decided to break the "curse" by chanting as he circled a small bonfire. Some say that's what brought victory to the Astros in the next game.

Over the decades, many other pitchers have used a variety of rituals to keep luck on their side. Bob Owchinko, once with the Oakland Athletics, always wanted the resin bag in the same place when he was on the mound—it had to be a little to the right and behind him. Rituals with the resin bag are important to today's stars also. One may have to tap it two or three times for luck. Another might have to toss it over a shoulder. Still another might just pick it up to check it out before each game starts.

Mark "the Bird" Fidrych, a popular Detroit Tigers pitcher, became known for his antics with bubble gum, chewing and blowing carefully controlled bubbles as part of his game routine. But he was more often described as the pitcher who talked to the baseball. When he was on the mound, he looked like he was reciting an incantation, helping to spur the baseball on. He also took special care of the mound, patting it firmly and carefully into place.

Al Hrabosky, who was short relief for the St. Louis Cardinals, Kansas City Royals, and Atlanta Braves, used to make his own magic to improve his game. Called the "Mad Hungarian," Hrabosky would grow a Fu Manchu mustache every season so that he would look as menacing as possible. Before pitching, he would walk behind the mound, turn his back on the hitter, and meditate intensely. Then he would slam the ball into his glove, walk to the mound, and glare at the batter. If that did not put a jinx on the guy at bat, Hrabosky figured nothing else would.

A current star, pitcher Dwight Gooden, uses a rap to present his tough image and deliver his hex. The rap describes his "Changeup, fastball/Slider, curve," and concludes with the challenge, "Step up to the plate/If ya got the nerve."

Clothes Conscious

Shoes, socks, shirts, shorts, hats—various types of clothing are symbols of good luck for many baseball players. Although no one will say for sure that baseball great Hank Aaron was superstitious, he wore the same pair of shower shoes for twenty years. They are displayed at the Milwaukee County Stadium where Aaron once played—first as a Brave (when the stadium was the home of the National League team) and later as a Brewer.

Some ballplayers wear a particular brand of shoes while they're winning, then switch to another brand if they lose. Pete Vukovitch wore two different brands at the same time—one brand on the right foot, another on the left. Others have worn the same socks for luck, never washing them during a series of wins.

Milwaukee Brewers left-handed pitcher Paul Mirabella wears the same undershirt for games. At the beginning of the 1989 season, the shirt was six years old. "It's nothing but holes—in the stomach, on the shoulder—and so thin you can see through it. But Mirabella has to wear it," the Brewers' equipment manager says, adding that "a lot of guys wear the same underclothes for luck."

A Los Angeles Dodgers hitter agrees, explaining, "If I'm in a hitting streak, I wear the same undershirt and shoes until the streak ends." An Atlanta Braves player wore the same undershirt for so many seasons it was "ragged out," hardly enough cloth left to keep it together.

Caps and batting helmets can be important good luck talismans. A player might refuse to take his hat off during a game, even wearing it under a batting helmet. If he's pitching well, Bill Wegman insists on wearing the same hat even though it may be streaked with sweat, pine tar, and dirt. Because of a long string of victories, pitcher Vida Blue wore the same baseball cap whenever he was on the mound. After three seasons, the cap became so dirty and decrepit that he was threatened with suspension if he didn't destroy it. He finally gave in, but he held a special ceremony for his cap, burning it on the field.

Before Terry Francona became part of the Brewers regular roster, he swore by the batting helmet he had used in spring training. Like other players he was issued a new helmet for the playing season, but when he had gone without a hit for eight times at bat, he pleaded with the equipment manager to "give me back my old helmet." Francona wore the beat-up helmet in the next game, which was against the Texas

Rangers, and in a late inning he got the first hit off Nolan Ryan, stopping a no-hitter.

"Bless" the Bats (and the Gloves, Too)

Baseball gloves and bats are also shrouded with superstition. One player believes his glove brings good luck if it's rubbed all over with a colored marking pencil. Some players insist on saving their "game gloves" for competition; using them for practice would be bad luck. Many players feel it is unlucky to part with their gloves. Kansas City outfielder Amos Otis insisted on using the same glove for his entire career. The glove became ragged but it was his lucky piece of equipment.

Some big-league fielders have been known to drop their gloves very carefully before going to bat. The fingers have to point toward their team's dugout. An improperly placed glove could bring bad luck.

Over the years, some players have believed their bats were only good for a certain number of hits or home runs. It would be a real jinx to lend a bat to a fellow player before the hits or runs had been "used up." Another jinx is a split bat. It has to be discarded quickly—out of sight and out of mind. And no bats should be allowed to lie across each other—a sure hex.

Between seasons a bat might be buried to preserve it. Players have been known to pass prayer beads, crosses, dried chicken bones, polished stones, rabbit feet, and other symbolic items over their bats for luck. A bat might be prayed over, placed in a chapel or other religious setting, or rubbed with a lucky compound, ranging from motor oil to tobacco juice. Many players insist on placing their bats in specific slots in the bat rack—the upper left-hand corner, for example. Wade Boggs always places his bat in the middle slot.

During a game, some hitters will not use a bat that has been in batting practice. Others insist on using only a certain kind of bat. Milwaukee outfielder Rob Deer didn't start his career that way (he used every kind of bat), but he broke his wrist during a recent season and was out for six weeks. When Deer came back he used a Worth bat that he feels brought him luck. Now it's the only kind he'll use, "and hard to get," the equipment manager says.

Many top hitters have been known to cuddle and caress their bats, almost as if the sticks had lives of their own. Some clean and polish their bats after each game, and a few store their bats in locked cases. Some players sleep with their bats. In short, when they are doing well, top hitters want to make sure nothing happens to their wood or aluminum. It's the same as protecting their luck or good fortune.

★ 2 ★

DEFYING FATE
ON THE FOOTBALL FIELD

Are the big "bad" Bears from Chicago superstitious? Judge for yourself. During several successful seasons, the team's linebackers always dressed an hour before the game and then sat together in the stands. Nothing strange about that, you could say. But the linebackers refused to vary their routine because that might change their luck. At one time, nearly all of the Bears players maintained a pregame ritual inside the locker room. Each player who visited the "boys' room" carried a program. Was it unlucky to go without one?

Individual rituals have been common, such as putting on a uniform in a set pattern or sitting on the bench in a certain spot before each game. Former defensive tackle Alan Page, for example, always sat at the 50-yard line just before the game started.

During the 1970s, Bears tackle Dan Jiggetts, who is now a TV sports commentator, made sure he taped the colors of the opposing team on the knuckles of his gloves. Doug Buffone, former linebacker, followed a most disrupting routine. He felt he had to throw up before every game, but not because of a nervous or upset stomach. Buffone did it for luck!

Ted Albrecht, a tackle/guard, began a good luck routine in the locker room and completed it on the field. Albrecht carefully placed a penny in his helmet while he was still dressing for the game. But on the field, he handed the penny over to the equipment manager, who taped the good luck coin to his cigarette lighter. The penny could then stick around to cast its charm over the game.

During the past few seasons, the Bears defensive end, Steve McMichael, has made a pregame ritual of walking onto the field while still in his street clothes. Teammate Tom Thayer always has to be the first guy in the locker room on game day. Dan Hampton, a defensive tackle, crawls under a trainer's table and stays there for at least a half hour, while another teammate drapes a towel over his head five minutes before game time. Center Jay Hilgenberg has to have the equipment manager (and no one else) pull down his T-shirt sleeves so they will not bunch up under his jersey, and he insists on a certain type and length of shirt. If a shirt is too long, Hilgenberg cuts it off at the bottom. It could be that these pregame exercises really do help players set the stage for a win.

Payton Patches

Number one runner Walter Payton wore a sling-type baseball sock over sweat socks rather than the regulation tube socks used by other Bears players. The stripes and colors of the baseball socks were in line with the National Football League (NFL) equipment guidelines, but that was not quite the case with his game pants.

During his many years with the NFL, Payton wore only two pairs of pants. He refused new ones. New jerseys were okay, but Payton insisted that his pants should be patched—for luck. No one dared suggest what might happen if the patch did not hold during the game!

Gearing Up for Game Day

Certainly, the Chicago Bears are not the only superstitious football players. During the 1970s, a Dallas Cowboys defensive end absolutely had to eat two hot dogs before he would go out onto the field. It was once a ritual for the Oakland Raiders to wait until running back Mark van Eeghen had burped before the team would leave the locker room.

On many teams there is usually a player who is very careful about who tapes him. He may insist on a certain trainer and a specific time and pattern for taping. Some players may be superstitious about the way they lace up their rib protectors or the order in which they put on their uniforms. Others tape medallions inside their shoes. Some years ago a defensive tackle for the Tampa Bay Buccaneers put a dime under the inner sole of his shoe before each game. Without the coin, he felt he was "just asking for bad luck."

Linebacker Ervin Randle of the Buccaneers writes the word "viper" on his shoes for good luck. "I've been doing that since high school," he says. "It may not have anything to do with my success, but I feel better knowing the word is on the back of my shoes."

On road trips, one former Rams quarterback always used to sleep in a bed next to the hotel or motel door—his "lucky place." A former Rams wide receiver, Harold Jackson, followed a carefully ordered pregame sequence when he lived on the West Coast. The first thing in the morning, before a game, he attended vesper services. He always drove the same route to the stadium and parked in the same place, making sure he was in his spot an hour before game time. Jackson also insisted on wearing white shoes—not the Rams' color—because he believed he ran faster in white.

For his stint with the San Francisco Forty Niners, Ray Wersching created his own style of ritual. Whenever he tried for a field goal, he never glanced at the goal posts. That would be the same as looking for bad luck. Instead, he depended on quarterback Joe Montana to guide him to the hashmarks, the inbound lines near the center of the field. While heading for his spot, Wersching called for Montana to "Help me, help me!" One of the trainers said the routine was "like a blind man trying to cross a busy intersection," but in this case it was truly comical—and pure superstition.

One of Montana's teammates, defensive end Dwaine Board, always turned the T-shirt that he wore under his shoulder pads inside out. That way the words "Forty Niners" on the shirt were against his skin for luck.

The Old Numbers Game

Like baseball players, many football stars have insisted on using lucky equipment in a game. If players have done well wearing certain shoulder pads, hip pads, or helmets, the gear is going to stay with those players to assure good luck. But numbers are equally, if not more, important.

Of course most athletes, whatever their game, stay away from number 13. Triskaidekaphobia it's called— a fear of 13. A majority of people worldwide believes the number is unlucky. The belief stems from ancient times. Some historians speculate that primitive people looked on 13 with fear because at first it had no real identity. People could name and count numbers only from one to twelve. Beyond that, numbers had to be identified by a combination of names for previous numbers. Thirteen, then, was a kind of outsider, not in harmony with the original group of identified num-

bers. Over the ages, 13 became more threatening,
symbolizing evil and death.

Yet there were ancient peoples like the Mayan and
Aztec societies who thought 13 was a divine or sacred
symbol. Thirteen also has generally been a fortunate
number for the United States—the nation began with
13 colonies. Check out the U.S. dollar bill—it's covered with symbolic 13s, from 13 stars to an eagle with
13 tailfeathers, holding 13 arrows and an olive branch
with 13 leaves.

Today, a few sports figures will ask to wear 13 on
their uniforms as a way of defying bad luck. More
often, though, players pick jersey numbers designed
to bring them luck. Double numbers are popular as
lucky symbols—they seem to spell trouble for the
opposition. Perhaps that's why the number 77 always
belonged to the powerful Red Grange of 1920s fame
and why Alan Page claimed number 88.

When a pro is traded, he usually wants his old
number to go with him. Losing it could make him feel

he is going to lose out on his luck, too. If a player finds someone else on the team is wearing "his number," what then? Sometimes he can convince a teammate to trade, or perhaps he'll settle for his old number turned backwards (23 for 32, for example) or maybe split up a lucky number like 39, wearing part of it—3—on a home jersey and the other half on the jersey used for road trips.

The number 43 on the jersey of one amateur-league player turned out to be a lucky one. Apparently, the quarterback's father had picked a series of numbers for the New York State Lottery, with the final one being 44. But at the last minute, the father Pat Consalvo decided to change the 44 to 43 because that was the number on his son's football jersey. Good luck? No doubt about it, Consalvo will tell you. He won $30 million.

Coaches, too, might do well to consider some lucky numbers. At Notre Dame, legendary coach Knute Rockne won his first national championship in his third season. Four other coaches did the same: Frank Leahy, Ara Parseghian, Dan Devine, and most recently, Lou Holtz won the national championship in the 1988 season—Holtz's third with the team.

Big Ten Rituals

Many professional football players began some of their rituals when they were playing for college teams. At Indiana University, football players have reported a variety of superstitious practices. One said he laced his shoes with a new pair of strings for luck before every game. Another reported that he repeated the ditty "Step on a crack and you break your mother's back" to make sure he did not step on the boundary lines coming off the field.

One former player describes a rather complex routine. He explains that on game day "I got up and showered, but I did everything in reverse order. Instead of soaping first, then shampooing my hair, and finally brushing my teeth, I brushed first and soaped last. At breakfast, I stuck to the same menu I always had before a game. Then I went back to my room and cleaned it up because a messy room meant I'd have a messy day on the field. When I got ready to go to the stadium, I wouldn't wear anything with the other team's colors. But I always wore a ring. Without it I'd have bad luck I figured."

Another IU player—call him Gary—had an even more elaborate ritual. He was the first to arrive at the stadium for any practice session so that he could dress in an unhurried fashion, putting on his uniform in a certain order, without interference. Then he would put on his shoes, making sure he got the left one on first. It had to be that way for practice. On game day, however, he would reverse the order. The procedure was essential, he believed, for good luck.

Once dressed, Gary would sit in the stands for a while. He would make sure, though, that he did not pick a spot where he had been before. It was bad luck not to change the place where he relaxed for a few minutes before the drills got under way.

On the morning of a game, Gary would follow a careful ritual he had established. At the team breakfast, he never finished a glass of milk or orange juice, filling it up when it was almost empty. After he ate, he called home so his parents could wish him good luck. Then he took a shower and sat in the locker room for a while "just spacing out." Dressing for the game, he would ask the trainer—the same person each time—to tape his ankles, right one first. After that, he put on his uniform, all except for his jersey. He never pulled it over his head until he went out for the pregame warm-ups. He had a special spot for the workout, and during the game, when he had to wait on the sidelines, he always stood between the 40- and 35-yard lines.

Whether in college or pro football, players try never to deviate from their lucky rituals. But there are exceptions. If something goes wrong in a game, it is not unusual for a player to change his routine—switch trainers, wear different clothes, eat different foods, develop a new daily schedule for himself. The idea is to change one's luck from bad to good.

Mascots Make Magic

As in baseball, mascots are important good luck symbols for many football teams. In 1987, the Denver Broncos adopted a black cat for a mascot. Although ancient Egyptians believed a black cat symbolized good fortune, most people today associate a black cat with bad luck on the way. Not only did the Broncos pick a black cat, they also selected a mascot that had wandered into the practice area on Friday the 13th, thought by many to be the unluckiest day of the year. But rather than accept a double whammy, the Broncos

seemed challenged by it. The team went on to win their next game.

It isn't hard to guess what kind of mascot guides the Miami Dolphins. Naturally, it's the sea mammal, the bottlenose variety. For centuries, sailors have considered the dolphin good luck and one of the most intelligent creatures of the sea. To harm a dolphin would be bad luck indeed. No doubt that's the idea the Miami team wants to put across to opponents.

Mascots are familiar sights in the amateur ranks. The Army has its goat. The Naval Academy has a mule. And of course the "luck o' the Irish" is embodied in the green and gold imp, the leprechaun. Images of the little fellow appear on homes, businesses, vehicles, and many other places around the University of Notre Dame campus in northern Indiana.

★ 3 ★

More
Team Magic

While Notre Dame teams lay claim to the luck of the Irish in the Midwest, the East Coast Celtics also have faith in their Irish heritage. The Boston pros wear the Irish green as well. Maybe that's part of what makes them one of the most successful basketball teams around.

Do the Celtics follow any rituals to help them maintain their good fortune? Perhaps players would deny any connection to sports magic, but the Celtics have a specific routine before the beginning of every game. Each season one player is designated to finish the warm-ups before the Celtics are introduced to fans in the Boston Garden. And that player never varies his particular warm-up shots, whether it happens to be a dunk shot or two free throws or a fancy layup.

Another National Basketball Association (NBA) team, the Chicago Bulls, decided to do something about their bad luck when they played against the Cleveland Cavaliers during the 1989 season. Before the division playoffs, the Bulls had not won a single game over Cleveland. Both teams made it to the playoffs, so every member of the Bulls changed his regular white shoes with red trim to all black shoes. In addition, Doug Collins, the coach, wore black sneakers, (and white socks), even though he usually dressed in a dapper suit for each game, and general manager Jerry Krause decided to wear the same suit for each series game. Did it work? Almost. The Bulls won the series against Cleveland 3–2, and went on to be victorious over the New York Knicks. But they lost the final series against the Detroit Pistons. (So what can you say? Better luck next time?)

Personalized Magic

Individual players have their own brand of magic, too. One Milwaukee Bucks star claimed the first seat—his lucky spot—on the bench whenever his team played. A Detroit Pistons center always practiced his free throws at a specific time during warm-ups. An Indiana Pacers forward has to eat two candy bars—either Snickers or Kit Kats—before a game. The Celtics' Larry Bird rubs his hands on his shoes before going onto the court.

Here's a trivia question for you. What did basketball star Wilt Chamberlain wear for luck? He always wore a rubber band on his right wrist. He also wore the number 13, regardless of the team he played with. For Chamberlain, 13 was a lucky number.

Several Houston Rockets players have copied Chamberlain's practice of wearing a rubber band bracelet. But an Indiana Pacers guard prefers tape on his left wrist—he covers it with two sweatbands.

Former Houston forward, Ed Ratleff, didn't wear anything on his wrist. Instead, he always wrapped a piece of string around his ring finger. The string replaced a ring that had brought him luck in a tight game.

What about college and high school players? Are they as likely to follow superstitious practices as the pros? That seems to be the case. One example was cited in *Women's Sports and Fitness*. As Linda Kay wrote: "Harlem Globetrotter Lynette Woodard always wore two identical wristbands on the same arm when she played at the University of Kansas."

Beyond that, two Canadian psychologists surveyed high school and college basketball players in Alberta, where basketball is a popular school sport. Their findings showed that superstitions were widespread among the 310 interviewees. Regular players were likely to take part in some pregame rituals and those connected with shooting free throws. The study also indicated that those who regularly attended religious services took part in prayer-related rituals before games, and had more superstitious beliefs than the rest of the players. Yet the researchers found so many variations among players that they could draw no definite profile of a superstitious athlete.

If basketball players develop magical practices in college or high school, they tend to carry these into the professional arenas. A well-known example is Chicago Bulls guard Michael Jordan, who wears basketball shorts that are about two inches longer than those worn by the rest of the team. The extra length covers his old playing shorts from his North Carolina days, which he wears for luck.

Adrian Dantley (formerly with the Detroit Pistons and now with the Dallas Mavericks) follows a game ritual that has never varied from his days as a high school basketball player. When he's at the free-throw line preparing to shoot, he turns and twists the ball, fondles, and rolls it. "You can't really describe it—you have to see it to believe it," says one observer.

Basketball Coaches and Their Capers

What basketball coaches wear makes a big difference in a game, so they say. Blazers, sweaters, pants, shirts, and ties seem to be important to court good luck. Don Nelson, a former Milwaukee Bucks coach, put on a lucky tie that looked like a fish. A famous University of Kentucky coach, Adolph Rupp, always wore a particular shade of brown suit. A Connecticut coach was partial to a hand-knit sweater from Italy that he wore for luck. The University of Indiana coach Bobby Knight always wears a red sweater with the lower ribbing rolled up beyond his waistline.

Notre Dame's Digger Phelps used to wear a carnation in his suit coat lapel, but he has changed his image and is now wearing informal attire. Why? Because he says his teams are different from those of the past (and perhaps he needs to change their luck?).

One University of Kansas coach had to have a white

handkerchief in the breast pocket of his blazer or sports jacket. John Thompson, coach of the Georgetown team, always hangs a towel over his shoulder. Other coaches have been known to collect lucky hairpins (there's that old superstition again!), or pat their players for luck.

Stan Albeck has been described as one of the most superstitious coaches in the NBA. His superstitions came to light during his first years (early 1980s) with the San Antonio Spurs. Like his hero, former coach Rupp, Albeck began to wear brown clothing for luck. Cowboy boots were a must. If his team lost, he put aside the blazer or sports coat he'd worn and found another for the next game.

Albeck also was faithful to a number of other superstitious routines. It was important to read every billboard along the highway from his home to the sports arena. If a sign had been removed, he saw that as a bad omen and tried not to look. Before a game Albeck never watched team warm-ups. That, too, was bad luck.

In Indiana where basketball season is called Hoosier Hysteria, high school basketball coaches are known for lucky wearables. One southern Indiana coach wore a pair of hand-stitched, patchwork pants for a twenty-seven-game winning streak. Another Hoosier coach wore Rupp brown. But when his brown suit wore out, the Austin, Indiana, coach switched to a green suit. It too became threadbare, so it was on to blue blazers for luck.

Perhaps the state of Ohio runs a close second to Indiana in basketball fever. One Ohio coach, Paul

Walker, wore the same suit during the longest winning streak in high school basketball history. It all began during the 1950s, when one of the stars on the Middletown, Ohio, team was Jerry Lucas, who later went on to national fame. For three seasons the Middies, as the team was called, chalked up seventy-six consecutive wins, and people all across the state talked about the Middie Magic.

Coach Walker may also have set a record with the number of times he wore his pants thin and had to have a tailor patch the seat and restitch the weakened seams—all in the name of Lady Luck. As Walker continued to coach the Middies over nearly three decades, he added a lucky tie and hat to his wardrobe. He wore the red hat going back and forth to the gym.

Before every game he had his team stretch out on the gym floor, face down, in a circular pattern, the player's hands touching in the middle. Then as Walker instructed his team to prepare mentally for the game, he gave each one a good luck pat on the back. He followed that routine without fail all of his coaching career.

During a winning streak, Walker also insisted that his players wear the same warm-up suits. "No sense changing the luck," he'd say. In fact he believed that "if you have success with something you might as well keep using it until the magic quits working for you."

Hockey Habits

Following a lucky routine is a philosophy of many a hockey coach, manager, and player. During the 1970s, a Toronto Maple Leafs coach believed in the power of pyramids. He pasted pictures of pyramids under the Toronto bench to bring strength and glory to the team.

One Chicago Blackhawks coach of long ago, Pete Muldoon, put a hex on his team. It was hardly sportsmanlike behavior. But Muldoon wanted to get even because he had been fired by the owner of the team. "You'll never win the Stanley Cup," Muldoon declared in a fit of temper. He meant it as a jinx. It took more than thirty years for the Blackhawks to get out from under the Muldoon curse, as they called it. They finally won the Stanley Cup in 1962.

In recent times, the former Minnesota North Stars manager Lou Nanne, who also had been a popular team player, was so superstitious that his rituals became extreme. For example, as manager he would sit in the press box without moving if the Stars were winning. But if the other team scored he would find a different seat, circle it four times, then sit down to watch the next play. He followed many other rituals as well, trying always to repeat patterns in dress and actions that he believed had helped his team win.

As a team the Philadelphia Flyers have long depended on the powerful singing voice of the late Kate Smith. In the past Smith was called upon to sing her popular rendition of "God Bless America" during pregame ceremonies, and the tean went on to win. After Smith died, the Flyers played a tape recording of Smith's rendition rather than switching to another singer.

Another team, the New York Rangers, gave credit to a special drink for their long streak of wins during the early 1950s. Apparently, a fan and restaurant owner created a drink called a Magic Elixir, which he gave to all the players. After drinking the "potion" the team went on to win game after game. Not only the Rangers believed in the magic qualities of the drink. Their opponents, the Toronto Maple Leafs, once tried to steal the elixir from the Rangers, hoping of course to gain the advantage with the lucky brew.

For many players a common practice on game day is doing everything exactly as it was done on the day of a previous win. That could mean getting out of bed the same way, opening or closing a particular window, eating the same meals, wearing the same coat or sweater to the rink, or following the same route to the game. As one manager explains: "It's a matter of being very precise about repeating actions that a player believes could bring a win on the playing field."

Individual quirks are common, too. Hockey great Wayne Gretzky has to tuck his uniform jersey into just one side of his pants—the right side. A Minnesota North Stars player reported that he tries to turn his luck around by changing gloves, headband, and wristbands after a period when he has not played well.

During the 1980s, at least three hockey players—a Vancouver Canuck's defenseman, a Boston Bruins center, and a New York Rangers forward—chose to wear the number 13 on their jerseys, calling it a switch on Fate. Other oddities include a player who had to eat a bag of popcorn before a game and the one who always had to see a movie and eat a chocolate sundae the night before. Several players insist on having their hockey sticks wrapped with tape from a new roll.

Some players have to stop a certain number of shots during warm-ups or skate a specific warm-up route. One player has to jog around the training table before going out on the ice; another insists on being the last person to leave the locker room.

Most players make sure that hockey sticks do not lie crossed—anywhere. Like crossed baseball bats, it's bad luck. In fact, any game equipment (such as cue sticks) should not be crossed; such actions bring misfortune, according to ancient beliefs. But ironically, crossed fingers are supposed to ward off hexes of all kinds.

Hockey players also must avoid saying "shutout" in the locker room. Again, the superstition is similar to one in baseball—staying mum about a "no-hitter" in the making. It could be bad luck to mention the possibility of a sh—(don't say it!). Once a player on a Yale University team disregarded this taboo and the team lost its 4–0 advantage within minutes.

Phil Esposito (who was the New York Rangers general manager) was one of the most superstitious hockey players. Through his long career as a star center, Esposito's magical practices became legendary. His elaborate routine involved not only putting on his uniform and gear in a pattern that never varied but also wearing a black turtleneck sweater that had brought him good luck early in his career. He was noted for arranging his equipment in a specific order. His gloves had to be placed one on each side of the hockey stick with the tips of the gloves and stick perfectly aligned. A pack of fresh gum was always next

41

to him, and he never played a game without saying his prayers as the national anthem was played.

Most hockey players believe they should tap the goalie on his shin pads before a game. One defenseman used to tap the goalie and insist that the goalie tap back. Without the return tap the defenseman believed he would not play well. Another defenseman always tried to be the last person to talk to the goalie before the game started.

Goalies themselves may be more superstitious than other players on a team. A New York Islanders goalie, for example, thought it was bad luck for anyone to touch him or his equipment before a game. A Canucks goalie once had a sock with two holes in it that he wore to do well during a game.

One former Montreal Canadiens goalie, Ken Dryden, wrote in his book *The Game,* that he was almost a prisoner to his superstitions and felt "helpless to do anything about it." During his playing days, Dryden had a pregame ritual that involved taking utmost care *not* to look when inspectors were checking to see that the goal lights were working. In warm-ups he had to have the first shot. The puck had to "strike the boards to the right of my net between the protective glass and the ice." If that didn't happen, Dryden believed he would "play poorly," he wrote.

A Philadelphia Flyers goalie noted that he gets dressed and puts on his equipment exactly the same way before each game: left skate first and then his right; left pad and then right pad. Everything is left, right, left, right. What happens if the routine gets mixed up? He will take his equipment off and start all over again.

Soccer Superstitions

Soccer has become increasingly popular in the United States but is more widely played in European, Latin American, and African countries. Some involved in the sport say it is not as tied to good luck routines as other team games. Yet, the Argentine star Pelé was said to be "obsessed" with the number 10. Much of his life on and off the playing field centered on 10 and configurations of the number.

The New York Times reported several years ago that the Mwangeka soccer team from a village in western Kenya, Africa, called in a medicine man to put a curse on the goalkeeper of the opposing team. Perhaps that was the reason the Mwangeka team won 4–3.

In his book *Superstition and the Superstitious,* Eric Maple pointed out that when British soccer players enter the field they "religiously pass the ball from the oldest to the youngest player for luck, and the ball is frequently bounced precisely three times before the team takes up its position. It is also the custom to touch the goal posts for luck."

Mascots, from four-legged creatures to humans, are part of the magic rituals surrounding soccer. A young child might even become a mascot for some British teams. British soccer players also are prone to dressing for a game in ritualistic ways, particularly putting on the left boot first.

The left-foot-first ritual is a part of many athletes' routines, but the pattern is just the opposite of how

most people put on a boot, shoe, or sandal. World-wide, people usually begin with the right foot. Apparently, this practice can be traced to ancient Rome where it was considered proper to put the right foot forward first and to start out on the left foot meant bad luck. No one knows exactly why some athletes have turned that tradition around.

In the United States, one professional team, the Tampa Bay Rowdies, has readily admitted to superstitious practices. Over the years, shoes have been blessed with magical powers, that is if they have been treated properly. Several Rowdies have insisted that all shoes on the locker room shelf point inward; if not, they'd refuse to wear them. One player talked to his shoes. Another always had to place his right foot on the field first, while a teammate had to step on the field before he'd put on his game shorts. Several Rowdies have believed it was bad luck to put on game shirts until just before they walked onto the field.

What happens when superstitions just don't work for a team? Yale University soccer players came up with one solution. They lost so many games during the mid-1970s that players dropped many of their superstitious rituals in attempts to change their luck!

★ 4 ★

SUPERSTITIONS
IN GOLF, TENNIS,
RACQUETBALL, AND TRACK

Golf, or goff as it was called in antiquity, is one of the earliest games that involved hitting a ball with a club or bat. The game came on the scene in Scotland during the 1400s, more than a century after cricket became a popular sport. No one knows the exact origin of the game. But . . . perhaps goff was invented because of a commonly held belief that hitting a ball on the ground would somehow appease the gods of the earth and make crops grow.

However golf came about, modern golfers still seem to bow to the gods of the greens and fairways. And they try to coax (or force) magical properties onto their clubs and balls. There are players who believe it's a good omen to start out a tournament using only odd-numbered clubs. Many professional golfers refuse to play with the unlucky number 3 ball, unless it's for a practice session.

Magic Markers

It's a common practice for golfers to carry coins for luck, sometimes the same ones for each tournament. Perhaps it's a coin from a special collection or one sent by a fan. One golfer in the Ladies Professional Golf Association (LPGA) borrows coins from her caddy to put in her pocket for luck. Such famous golfers as Jack Nicklaus, Tom Weiskopf, and Lee Trevino have carried coins—usually lucky pennies or dimes.

Golfers frequently use coins to mark the ball, the spot on the green where the ball stopped so that it can be picked up and removed from another golfer's putting line. This might not be considered a superstitious practice except when a golfer makes sure to use the same coin each time. One pro who used a penny for marking always had to place the coin heads up.

Bugs are a mark of good luck for an LPGA golfer. She refuses to kill insects if they happen to be in her path on the golf course. Perhaps stepping on a bug is linked with squashing her luck in the game.

Working Amateur Magic

Listen to amateur golfers—those who play for the fun and frustration of the game—and nearly all will swear that they are not superstitious. But then they go on to describe their own personal beliefs about the luck involved in golf and how they work their own personal magic.

Some golfers insist that certain clubs are lucky or that their clubs have to be in a certain order in their bags. Ask golfers about approaching a tee and one will

say it is unlucky to approach from the right side, another will say that the left side is bad luck, and most will say never never approach from the front.

"You have to place the ball on the tee with the name in line with the hole," says one golfer.

A second golfer disagrees: "You should place the ball on the tee so that you can clearly see the trade name or number on top."

"You have to use the same ball for an entire round— unless it's cut or something," says another.

"You have to be sure to take a new ball out of its wrapping before you get to a tee."

"Don't use a ball with a high number on it because that could cause you to have a high number of strokes for each hole."

"It's bad luck to take a club out of a bag and then change your mind and use another."

"You should never clean a golf ball if your game is going well."

"You should use the same color tees unless your game is poor—then you should change to a different color."

"You should never use a yellow tee—very bad luck!"

Color Coordinated

Yellow is a color that many golfers, whether amateur or pro, avoid. But most golfers pick a favorite color and make sure that their major pieces of clothing and gear are color coordinated. As one amateur golf champion in a women's tournament explains: "I always wear a golf glove that matches the pants, skirt, or top I have on; the hat has to match, too. An orange shirt calls for orange gloves and hat—and I've got 'em."

Another amateur golfer has to wear blue socks for luck. The charm of blue became apparent one day when he was supposed to play a major tournament but forgot to put on socks. He wore only sandals on his feet. So he had to rush to the store to buy some socks, which happened to be light blue in color. He won that tournament, "so it was just natural to wear those socks for competition until they were thin and full of holes," he explains. "But I've bought more blue socks and have worn them for golf ever since."

Even golfing pros are known for lucky colors. Green seems to be the most common. But Lee Trevino wears red—red socks and a red shirt at every tournament. Trevino obviously considers the color lucky. However, Byron Nelson, a tournament champ of years past, hated red. He refused to use a ball with any red markings on it. Bad luck of course.

Tennis Rituals

Color superstitions also affect many players on the tennis courts. Like golfers, some tennis players refuse to wear anything yellow because it could be a harbinger of misfortune. A top tennis pro of the 1970s felt he would lose a match if he wore anything blue. Another hated green . . . and on it goes.

Simply avoiding a color is not enough to ward off bad luck, however. A number of tennis stars, as with athletes in other sports, have worn the same outfits for every competition during a tournament, believing the outfits bring them luck. Many tennis players wear or carry talismans—lucky charms, tokens, or, as Jimmy Connors did, a note from his grandmother inside his sock.

People from nearly all walks of life have sworn that a four-leaf clover is a lucky charm, but one international tennis champion of long ago, Gerald Patterson, carried a four-leaf clover that once belonged to Abraham Lincoln. Patterson claimed that he always won when he carried the clover, but when he lost or misplaced it, he was defeated in a match. He did not win again until he found his good luck clover.

Several of today's tennis stars wear copper bracelets, which are supposed to ward off bad luck and arthritis. A few insist on specific colors for wristbands to bring them luck. Other tennis stars—Lisa Bonder and Martina Navratilova among them—have worn lucky earrings.

Magic rituals are just as much a part of tennis as other sports. A common one is walking around the

outside of the court when changing sides. Many players step over lines when going on to the court to serve. They also make sure that a letter or symbol on a racket faces the "right" way and may refuse to use "unlucky" balls (those responsible for a let or fault). Some tennis players change rackets in order to change their luck in a match. Others must bounce the ball a certain number of times before serving.

What happens before a match? Do tennis players, like other athletes, follow pregame routines? Yes indeed, although many don't think of themselves as superstitious. As a university student, a member of a women's varsity tennis team, explained:

I'm not afraid to walk under a ladder, and I don't get bent out of shape when a black cat crosses my path. But I do have a certain way I prepare for a match. Like, I always wear an old pair of shoes and a comfortable outfit. I would never wear a brand new pair of tennis shoes or new clothes. And I wear a bracelet I won in a paddle tennis tournament while in high school. And I guess I do eat the same thing before a match—a double cheeseburger, fries, and a shake. Maybe those are superstitions, but I think I just do these things to psych up for competition.

In the professional ranks, John McEnroe is said to have a specific pattern for shaving prior to semifinals. Björn Borg refused to shave when he competed in the Wimbledon tournament, and once he was on his way to a match he would never go back to his hotel room. If he forgot something he would send someone else to get it.

Many tennis stars try to stick to the same pregame menu, as long as they are winning. But food from the gods is likely to change should misfortune befall a player.

Tennis champ Greg Holmes follows a "right-sided" superstition because he always seats himself in a chair farthest to the right and puts his equipment bag on his right. He starts a match with two bands on his right wrist, but after the first game he puts a band on his left wrist.

One of the most persistent rituals was followed by a past tennis star, Arthur Larsen, who had to tap his racket on everything he passed. Perhaps this tap-tap routine came from a superstition that goes back to the time when people tapped or knocked on tree trunks to ask for good fortune from the good spirits thought to be inside. But for extra assurance Larsen knocked or tapped on more than wood. His racket did a quick tap dance on metal chairs and posts, nets, and many other objects. He even tapped on his doubles partner for luck. Is it any wonder he became known by the nickname "Tappy"?

Another tennis champ of the past, Helen Wills, believed that she had to put on her left shoe first. Putting the right shoe on before the left shoe would be bad luck. She knew this was a superstitious routine and once tried to change the pattern, putting her right shoe on first. The result? You guessed it—she lost her match, and later claimed that changing her routine had made her so uncomfortable that she was unable to concentrate.

More Rituals with Racquets

Racquetball players have more in common with tennis players than just hitting balls with racquets. According to a feature in *National Racquetball*, many top pros and amateurs in the game "practice a variety of . . . rituals before and after their matches with religious intensity." As with many other athletes, wearing the same outfit for every match or a favorite color is expected to cast a lucky glow. The common superstition of dressing the left-right way fits racquetball players, too. Lucky necklaces, religious medals, coins, shoelaces, unwashed wristbands, and other charmables accompany players on the racquetball court. And finally, players follow prematch routines similar to those of other athletes, such as eating the same meal before each competition or insisting on the same locker for a tournament.

Player Charlie Garfinkel, author of the report on racquetball superstitions, noted that he's "not what you'd call superstitious." However, he wrote (obviously with tongue in cheek): "Before a match I prepare psychologically by fondling my hundreds of trophies, medals, and silver pieces. If I don't read at least seven of my scrapbooks before any given match, I don't feel as if I'm ready to play. . . . If any of my shirts, jackets, headbands, or a pair of sneakers that says The Gar on them are stolen, this is a bad omen. It could even mean that my opponent will score between ten or twelve points, rather than his usual seven to nine."

Tracking Lady Luck

Most noncontact sports require intense concentration, and track is no exception. For some track stars, preparing for an event involves a routine that will encourage a favorable outcome. A British marathon runner used to listen to his favorite musical group The Who for an hour before each race. He said he had seen the group perform once and had won a race after that, so he felt that the group's music helped him prepare to win.

Although she had denied to reporters that she is superstitious, track star Jackie Joyner-Kersey has to eat chicken before every meet. The prerace diet for an Alabama marathon runner, Sue King, and a triathlon champ, Joanne Ernst, has been pancakes. Ernst also has worn the same earrings for every competition. Other runners tie their shoes in specific ways or, like some athletes in other sports, insist on wearing the same underwear whenever they compete.

Alan Woods, an amateur hurdler and member of a winning relay team in the Midwest, admitted that he was particularly superstitious about numbers. "I had to have a number that when divided into one hundred would give an even number," he says. He also had to wear a St. Christopher's medal, a common practice among athletes in many different sports, perhaps because St. Christopher is the patron saint of travel. Woods always dropped his medal over his shoulder with his right hand, placing it in back "so it wouldn't bounce around and hit me in the face while I ran, but would still be there for luck," he explains. "In the starting blocks, I had a strict ritual. I kicked my right leg straight up in the air and shook it. I made sure there were no pebbles where I put my hands. Then I placed my index finger parallel to the starting line and was ready for the start."

Luke Fahey, a university track star who excelled in pole vaulting said that he also focused on his St. Christopher's medal before a competition. "I wore the medal all the time except when I was competing in sports. Before a meet, I'd get dressed and try to separate myself from the rest of the team. Then I slowly and carefully took off my medal and put it in a box. I tried to treat the medal like I'd seen a priest handle the Host during a Sunday service. That helped me to relax and stay calm."

★ 5 ★

HORSE AND AUTO
RACING RITUALS

Perhaps no other domesticated animal has been more prized than the horse. Many ancient people believed horses were godlike, connected to the forces of good and evil, life and death, good luck and misfortune. Black horses usually signified death, but over the centuries some Europeans developed the belief that riding a black horse brought good luck. Others believed that a white horse was lucky. On the other hand, some have contended that seeing a white horse was a bad omen. No matter what color the horse, braiding its tail was a way to keep evil spirits at bay.

Lucky Horseshoes

No one is sure when the first iron horseshoes were used, but historians have noted that Celtic tribes in Britain were shoeing their horses before the Romans conquered their lands. People the world over are familiar with the good luck associated with the iron horseshoe. This belief may have roots in the worship of the Norse thunder god Thor, who deemed that iron was sacred.

Horseshoes have often been nailed over doors and under porches to assure good luck. But the iron shoe must be nailed with the open end turned up, otherwise the good luck could drain out or fall away from the points.

Mixing Horse Sense and Magic

Not surprisingly, many of the superstitions about horses and their iron shoes have carried over to racing. The first known horse races took place during the ancient Greek Olympiad. Greek athletes raced in horse-drawn chariots and on horseback. But the horses used in Greece were nothing like the stronger, faster-running horses that the Spanish bred centuries later. By the tenth century the English had also developed a breed of strong, swift horses, called Thoroughbreds, which could be used for racing. Horse racing was a standard form of entertainment at English festivals and fairs of the 1700s, and the sport was exported to America during the Colonial period.

At British and American racetracks nobody wanted a horse with four white feet. But it has long been considered a good omen to have a horse with one white hind leg and a white star on its forehead. Beware, though, of a horse that comes out of a stable with its left foot first. Good fortune rides with the horse that emerges right foot forward.

For many years, owners and breeders of racing horses have been wary of entering or going near a place where a horseshoe has been nailed on a wall or post upside down. Horse buyers also tremble at the thought of gathering at a sale where there are thirteen horses. Race horse owners would not think of changing their horses' names and do not want them photographed before a race, which would bring bad luck.

Jockeys prefer to keep their racing magic to themselves, because talking about their superstitions might dilute their effect. But there are some general superstitions that jockeys seem to maintain. Wearing a lucky suit on the way to a race is common. Riding boots should not hit the floor until it is time to put on a racing uniform, so jockeys store their riding boots on a shelf until race time. If riding boots are left standing on the floor, it is a symbol of being unhorsed, hardly a winning act for a jockey. Dropping a riding crop also dooms a victory.

No jockey ever wears another jockey's gear. It's bad luck. It's taboo. It's asking for problems. Don't even think about doing it, any jockey would warn. But jockey, Julie Krone, who has always done things her way, once wore the pants and boots of a friend who had been paralyzed by a fall from a horse. That was in 1984 and she won several races in one day. Since that time, Krone has been winning—her way, defying all jinxes—even defeating such famous jockeys as Bill Shoemaker.

Auto Racing Rituals

With the invention of the automobile, which pushed horses off roadways as a primary means of transportation, it was inevitable that auto racing became part of the sports scene. Steam cars in France raced between Paris and Rouen in the first recorded auto race, held in 1894. The next year, the first U.S. auto race from Chicago to suburban Evanston took place, with the winning car averaging 7.5 miles (12 kilometers) per hour.

Today professional auto racing is not only much faster but far more diversified than racing from one city to another. Road races now involve single-seat/open-wheel cars, sports cars, and four-seat racing cars. Races take place on oval tracks like the Indianapolis 500 speedway and tracks for stock car racing. Drag strip racing along a straight one-quarter mile course is also popular.

In spite of all the variations in auto racing, there is little doubt that some common superstitions surround this sport. Peanuts around a track are bad luck, although no one is sure why. News cameras can hardly be avoided, but some drivers still believe it's a bad omen to be photographed before a race—shades of a horse racing superstition.

Many drivers always get into their cars on the left side—Al Unser and Mario Andretti, Indianapolis 500 winners, and famous drag racer Shirley Muldowney among them. Muldowney, whose story was filmed in *Heart Like a Wheel* released in the mid-1980s, said that getting in on the left side of the car is just one of the consistent parts of her racing routine. "I don't consider it superstition really. I just do not like change. I am a creature of habit and before a race I check, double check, and triple check my car and equipment," Muldowney says.

However Muldowney also resists changing over to new equipment and gear. She has worn driving gloves until they fall apart, mending them with tape rather than buying a new pair. When she is testing a new car, she prefers to wear her old helmet, old uniform, and so forth, adding only one new thing at a time when necessary. "I've always thought that I followed this practice more for safety reasons," Muldowney says, "but perhaps, now that I think about it, you could say that's a superstition—to a degree."

Being consistent seems to be part of Bobby Rahal's magic practices also. Rahal won the Indy 500 race in 1986 after being a guest commentator on a TV show about the qualifying trials. At the request of his wife Debi, he accepted a similar invitation in 1989. Why? "I'm not that superstitious," he told a reporter, "but I'm covering all bases. Last time I did TV, I won." However, in 1989 the routine didn't work. Rahal's car had engine problems and he had to leave the race after lap fifty-seven.

Green is a No-Go

A green light has long signaled the start of a race, but the color has been a no-go for the paint on racing cars and most objects connected with auto racing in the United States. Not so in England, however. Green is the British national racing color (red is Italy's national color; Germans use silver cars).

Although the idea that the green goblins will getcha is a fading superstition in auto racing, many drivers and others connected with racing still have shades of the phobia. A story is told often about Mario Andretti refusing to sign autographs with a green pen, which he considers bad luck. No one is sure about the origin of the superstition, but it may stem from early racing days when green cars blended into the background of grass, shrubs, and trees near a track and thus were hard to see. In addition, some early drivers of green cars at the Indy 500 were killed or badly hurt in races.

As a result "green has been despised at the speedway," says an Indianapolis official. Oddly enough, the bleachers at the racetrack are painted green. But massive crowds pack the stands on race day, so the offensive color is covered up, perhaps burying the curse as well.

Nevertheless, over the years there have been plenty of instances when green has been expunged. During the 1950s, Troy Ruttman bought boxing shoes to drive in but discovered that the inside soles were green. So he tossed the shoes out. In 1968, Roger Ward, now retired, wore a green suit to the speedway, but people around him became so upset he had to change. In a similar instance that same year, the mother of racing brothers Bobby and Al Unser was invited to a drivers' meeting and wore a dress with a predominantly blue flower pattern. But there was a bit of green in the pattern and Mrs. Unser was asked to put on a different outfit.

Twenty years later, the green curse still bothered the Penske racing crew. The sponsor of the team, Miller beer, had a green stripe painted on their car to represent one of the colors on the beer label. Roger Penske argued that the stripe should be removed. But company policy seemed to take precedence over green phobias. Perhaps that had something to do with the bad luck that followed.

Penske driver Danny Sullivan, a 1985 Indy winner, was driving a green-striped car for the time trials before the 1989 Indy 500 race when the engine cover flew off. The car crashed into a wall, leaving Sullivan with a mild concussion, fractured right forearm, and bruised right foot. He wasn't expected to qualify for the big race. But he did and started twenty-sixth, moved up to twelfth place, and then the car's clutch went out, forcing Sullivan out of the race.

Two other Penske drivers also had to drop out of the 1989 Indy race. Al Unser's car suffered the same fate as Sullivan's, and the engine on Rick Mears's car failed. Talk about bad luck—!

Colors and Numbers that Count

While green must go underground in many auto races, blue seems to be a color with charm. Well-known National Association Stock Car (NASCAR) racer Richard Petty believed blue was his lucky color. He combined that with an attachment to the number 43, picked because it followed his father's racing car number. Racing champ Lee Petty always drove car 42.

Another believer in blue was Italy's famous Grand Prix racing driver, Alberto Ascari, who raced during the 1950s, but never without his lucky blue shirt and blue helmet. He also refused to go near the track on the thirteenth or twenty-sixth day of the month. In fact, he avoided any thing or place that had those numbers connected with them. Alberto felt he had good reason to follow the rituals. His father, also a racing hero, was fatally injured during a racing accident on the twenty-sixth day of the month. The elder Ascari died just seven weeks before his thirty-seventh birthday. Alberto was only seven years old at the time.

The younger Ascari never feared racing and began his career at an early age. He was considered one of the safest Grand Prix drivers, always in control, but exciting to watch. People flocked to see him wherever he raced, whether in Europe or the United States.

The 1955 Grand Prix season was a different story, however. Alberto Ascari was going through practice runs on a course that he knew almost stone by stone and certainly by every bend in the road. He was going into a third lap with an easy curve coming up when he suddenly jammed on the brakes—for no reason that anyone has been able to determine. In the next instant the car crashed and before an ambulance could get him to the hospital he died, just as his father had on the twenty-sixth day of the month, seven weeks prior to his thirty-seventh birthday. It was months later before people began to question why Alberto had not worn his blue shirt that fatal day. And what had happened to the blue helmet? It was in a repair shop getting patched up.

That much-maligned number 13 drives many racers to distraction. One driver, Louis Schneider, came to Indianapolis in the 1930s with the number 13 on his car, but the officials wouldn't let him race until he painted over the number. As luck would have it, he won the race.

Some drivers not only refuse to have anything to do with 13 but also multiples of the number. They will not stay in a hotel room that has a number (such as 76 or 94) that adds up to 13.

A few digits from 13, the number 17 has turned out to be an unlikely lucky number for one Daytona 500 racing driver, Darrell Waltrip. He had driven 17 Daytona 500s without a win. But on February 17 he became the Daytona 500 winner. At the time, his daughter was 17 months old. By the way, he also drives car number 17.

★ 6 ★

BOXERS AND WRESTLERS
BEAT BAD LUCK

"May the Good Duck be with you" the words on the sweatshirt read. The amateur boxer wearing the shirt was about to fight in a Golden Gloves competition. Not only had he put on his good luck shirt but he had also brought along a mascot, a stuffed duck, one of many in his collection. Why ducks? It seems they were a "natural," since the boxer, whose name is Daryll, was fondly called "the Duck"—a nickname Daryll's father (and trainer) created when his son was just a toddler.

Charm in the Square Circle

Many amateur boxers, and professionals as well, carry or wear lucky charms. Sometimes the charms are objects carried into the ring—dice, the proverbial rabbit's foot, or a religious medal. Some of the charms may be sewn inside trunks or be the clothing worn before a bout such as a robe or sweater, or even a special towel draped over the head. When Sugar Ray Leonard was an amateur boxer he taped a picture of his girlfriend (who became his wife) inside his sock for luck. Heavyweight champ Mike Tyson goes against tradition by not wearing championship white. Instead, he has worn black trunks and shoes and has refused to wear socks in the ring ever since his amateur boxing days.

Boxers sometimes carry agates, stones that have been valued as talismans for centuries. The stone is said to keep away the effects of the evil eye. A solid-colored agate supposedly makes any athlete unbeatable, and a black agate with veins of white running through it will help a person defeat his enemies.

Amateur and professional boxers have created colorful costumes to call attention to their arena entrances and also to surround themselves with a lucky aura. A fighter might wear trunks and a robe with appliqued four-leaf clovers. One lightweight professional boxer, Alvin "Too Sweet" Hayes, wore only yellow (turning the tables on cowardice?). His grand entrance was made in an outfit that included a yellow face mask, yellow satin shirt and trunks, and even yellow high top shoes.

Pre-bout rituals are some of the most important factors in determining what the outcome of a fight will be. Some boxers insist on shaking hands with a specific person—manager, trainer, or promoter—for luck. Others spend hours in privacy before a bout. Perhaps this is a good idea, because it's not unusual for a boxer to refuse to shower for days before a bout.

Many boxers have refused to allow women around during training, calling them "distractions" if not bearers of bad luck. Others wouldn't think of stepping into a ring without a prayer or meditation. As former world lightweight champion, Ray "Boom Boom" Mancini put it: "I always have a half hour of prayer to get a tranquil feeling so I can perform in a relaxed but aggressive state."

Former heavyweight boxing champion Muhammad Ali used plenty of hype while preparing for a bout. He often repeated rhymes that he had created to tout his special powers in a ritual designed to put a hex on opponents. But Ali also spent many days in physical and mental conditioning before a competition. Recently, he explained it this way: "Before a game or a boxing match, you must know inside yourself that you have done all that you possibly could to get in shape physically. If you worry about what you might have or could have done to be ready, then you will not be right in the head [for competition]."

"Prizefighters" of the Past

Boxers as a group probably rank next to baseball players as athletes most likely to take part in magical practices. However, prizefighters, as boxers were once called, of the early 1900s were more apt to admit their superstitions than would today's ring contenders. One story is told in *The Great American Sports Book* by George Gipe. According to Gipe, the welterweight Johnny Sumners followed a strict ritual between rounds. He'd "kneel on his corner clutching on old rag doll belonging to his daughter." An opponent once protested the action, saying Sumners was really smearing resin on his gloves. "The referee warned Sumners, but rather than give up his ritual, Sumners allowed himself to be disqualified," Gipe wrote.

Another prizefighter with steadfast superstitions was an Irish boxer, Tom Sharkey, who had a phobia about peacocks. He was certain they were bad luck. Once a fellow boxer and good friend, not knowing about Sharkey's intense fear of peacocks sent the Irishman several of the exotic birds to wish him well in a fight. Sharkey was so upset with the gift he wanted to return the peacocks, but he didn't want to hurt his friend's feelings. So against his better judgment Sharkey kept the gift, and lost his fight in the eleventh round.

Many boxers of the past feared bad luck if they saw a hat on a bed. The superstition apparently was born when one-time heavyweight champ Max Schmeling lost his title. Someone noticed after the bout that

Schmeling's friend had made a habit of dropping his hat on the fighter's bed. The hat was there the night of the loss, so a hat on the bed was henceforth declared bad luck.

Bob Fitzsimmons always said it was "bad stuff" to go into a dressing room after a defeated boxer. The well-known Gene Tunney never went into a ring ahead of his opponent, insisting it was bad luck. And many past pugilists believed that they should spit on their hands (and later gloves) to help bring about "telling blows."

Spitting in fact is practiced in many sports from organized baseball to recreational fishing. Those who spit may not be aware of the magic qualities saliva was once thought to possess. The ancients believed body fluids were sacred or were somehow connected with the supernatural. Through history, spittle has been used to anoint and to protect from evil.

The late Sugar Ray Robinson was a firm believer in dreams that he said foretold good luck or misfortune. In one instance described in his autobiography, he dreamt about his bout with Jimmy Doyle for the welterweight championship. "In the dream. . . I hit [Doyle] a few good punches and he was on his back, his blank eyes staring up at me. . . . The referee was moving in to count to ten and Doyle still wasn't moving a muscle. . . . I could hear people yelling 'He's dead. He's dead, . . .'" Robinson reported in his book. The next day he tried to call off the fight, but officials, priests, and other well-wishers convinced Robinson that it "was just a dream." Unfortunately, the bout turned out just as the dream had depicted.

Doyle died in the ring. After that Robinson said that he always heeded messages—premonitions, he called them—in his dreams.

Wrestling out of Bad Luck's Grip

Amateur wrestling is considered a secondary sport in most school programs, and unless wrestlers win Olympic competitions they rarely achieve fame. However, high school and collegiate wrestling "is the only real wrestling there is," claimed award-winning author John Irving in his essay included in the *Spirit of Sport*. Irving, a one-time wrestler, pointed out that amateur wrestling "should not be confused with those waddling melodramas acted out by so-called 'professional' wrestlers . . . beefy buffoons with their non-holds and their fake pain."

Because amateur wrestlers generally get little public attention, they may not be perceived as superstitious. But wrestlers are as prone to magical practices as any other athletes. One former wrestler said he "never looked at an opponent when he weighed in. It was not only bad luck but also gave the other guy a chance to try to psych you out by staring you down."

Another former wrestler (now a college coach) felt "there were probably a lot more superstitions in the fifties than now," and explained what went on when he was on a college team. "Everybody had a thing about food. We didn't know very much about how certain foods affected the body, so we thought that whenever the coach told us not to eat or drink something—popcorn and milk were no-no's—then that became a kind of superstition.

71

"We also had this ritual we went through before each match. The contenders would shake hands, pass each other, do a turn—each person had his own way, but it was always done the same each time. I never varied my routine. I felt like something would go wrong if I did."

Angelo Marino, who was a champion wrestler during the 1970s, admitted that he did "a lot of things to keep bad luck away. Like on the day of a match, I always wore my underwear inside out, with the tag showing. My uncle told me that a long time ago—said it would protect me if someone wished bad things would happen to me. I also wore my cross backwards, facing me, all day before a match. I left it on until right before my match. Before I wrestled I always made sure I had my towel—a white one with blue stripes. I put a little X on it in permanent ink, so that the mark stayed in the wash and I didn't get it mixed up with others. I folded the towel in a certain way and put a little blue star that my brother gave me on top of the towel when I put it in a drawer. Then before a match I'd put the towel at the top of the locker until I was ready to use it."

Today's Tricks

Are wrestlers different today? Well, perhaps. But an Ohio wrestler says, "I have to fold my clothes in a certain way. A lot of the guys, when they're getting ready for a match, just throw their clothes all over the place. It drives me crazy if my stuff is all messed up. Another thing, I always have to have someone in my corner—a friend, relative, somebody I know—when I compete. The person doesn't have to know anything about wrestling—just has to be there."

From a Tampa University wrestler comes this practice: "I don't ever watch the match before mine— might psych me to do poorly. And whenever I go into a gym where there's one of those exercise ladders, I always have to jump up and swing back and forth. If there isn't a ladder, then I'm okay. But once I didn't do my swinging routine on a ladder and I lost a match. So naturally every time I see a ladder, I do my thing."

Do wrestlers, like other athletes, have lucky clothes that they wear before or during a match? Of course, said a dozen collegiate wrestlers. Several wouldn't wrestle unless they wore their "winning" socks, which were seldom washed because that was bad luck. Some had shirts with good luck qualities. One wrestler

always wore "beat up" shoes that had brought him success. A couple of wrestlers wore tape on their wrists, even when they had no injuries; taping helped preserve a winning streak, they said. Another wouldn't wear a belt before a match. His reason? He could be "beaten with it."

★ 7 ★

BRINGING LUCK
TO BOWLING, BINGO,
AND OTHER INDOOR GAMES

Charlie McGarrahan rubbed his hands twice on his towel, picked up his bowling ball, gave it two quick slaps, and blew into the thumb hole twice. Then he made his approach, drew in a deep breath, and exhaled as he threw the ball down the alley. It was a simple routine, but Charlie followed it faithfully every time it was his turn to bowl. He is just one of thousands of amateur bowlers who have adopted various rituals designed to help them successfully deliver the ball and score.

Some bowlers always slap the bottom of their sliding shoes before they make an approach. Others go through a routine slap, dap of the resin bag on their hands and ball, rub the wall with their towel, twirl it a certain way—always the same gestures each time they prepare to bowl.

Peggy Swanson, who bowls in a weekly women's league, says her preparation routine is not quite as set. "I'm a sociable bowler and always talking to my teammates. Usually I don't care where I sit on the bench while waiting for my turn, but when I'm not scoring well, I don't socialize and I go sit by the scorekeeper to change my luck." Peggy adds that another woman on the team "gets up and walks once around a chair to change her luck in bowling."

Common Bowling Beliefs

Although many bowlers do not so readily admit to magical practices, they do feel compelled to "do what I have to do to score," as one person puts it. In other words, a routine or a set of habits becomes a necessary part of the bowling game; without it some bowlers feel jinxed and are unable to perform well.

Countless bowlers have body language designed to boost and guide the ball down the alley: raising doubled fists, jerking the arms back, twisting the hips, or even making flying leaps into the air. Some bowlers, though, turn their backs on the ball, walk away without looking at where the ball is headed. "If I don't look it will be a strike," one bowler says. "That's my superstition, I guess."

A common bowling belief is that a bowler's running score should never be marked on the scoresheet if she or he has a series of strikes going. Marking the scores "breaks the string," the saying goes. Team scorers also may draw in thick "fences" on the score pad to shut off open frames—when players fail to strike (X) or spare (/).

On the Pro Bowling Circuit

"Bowlers who make their living at the sport obviously take the game very seriously and have developed a variety of routines as they prepare to bowl," reports an official for the National Bowling Council (NBC). A member of the Professional Bowlers Association (PBA) agrees, saying typical actions include picking up a resin bag a certain way, toweling off the ball, and adjusting one's glasses. "Seasoned bowlers also tend to step onto the approach with the same foot every time," a PBA official says, adding that "there are occasions when bowlers will carry certain good luck items with them while bowling."

Championship bowler Pete McCordic is an example. Prior to the championship round in July 1988, McCordic revealed that he had been given a buckeye (a chestnut) by an Ohio fan who wished him good luck. McCordic kept the buckeye in his pocket while he was on national television, bowling and winning four straight matches for the tournament victory.

Another example is bowler Marshall Holman, one of the most successful professional bowlers in recent years. Holman has an elaborate routine that he goes through every time he gets ready to roll his ball. After taking his ball out of the rack, Holman taps a drying bag over the finger holes, takes his towel and rubs the ball completely to remove any oils on it, then he wipes the soles of each of his shoes—the right one first—before stepping up to the approach. "Holman does this every time in a very ritualistic manner and, I would assume, uses the time involved to clear his mind and plan his shot," the NBC official notes.

"Pre-shot rituals, along with post-shot body English, are a vital part of bowling," says Chuck Pezzano, Bowling Hall-of-Famer and columnist. "Call them silly, crutches, or whatever, bowlers who pump their balls six times before tossing them, or those who wipe off their balls with a towel an exact number of times, are doing what they must do. These rituals are definitely a help, if not in knocking the pins down, in getting mentally prepared to knock those pins over."

Even though some rituals help bowlers (as they do other athletes) concentrate on their shots or plays, the routines may be based in part on superstitious beliefs. As Pezzano explains: "Most bowlers in a hot scoring streak will make sure they wear the same shirt, same socks, same pants, same dress, or whatever until the streak dies down. Take the famed Johnny Petraglia, who always wears something red to ward off the bowling devils. But some bowlers hate red—wouldn't think of wearing it. Bowlers as a group prefer green. Wayne Webb is one. He's called the Green Machine because he usually wears green shirts, pants, socks, and shoes. To top it off, he uses a green bowling ball and a green towel to wipe his hands."

Other bowling champs have created outlandish or spectacular costumes to wear in tournaments. Guppy Troup buys two pairs of brightly colored, plain or patterned pants—but each pair is a different color or design. Then he has a tailor rip the pants apart and sew the right leg of one pair to the left leg of the

other. The result might be a pair of pants with one red leg and one green leg.

According to Pezzano, the "Liberace of the pro bowlers is Ernie Schlegel, who wears outfits made of exotic materials—bright silver or gold, satin and net— glittering with shiny buttons and stones."

A popular pro on recent tours, Amleto Monacelli, whose homeland is Venezuela, wears mismatched shoes when he competes. Apparently this happened by mistake during one tournament and Monacelli felt that the mixed pair—a red shoe and a white one— helped his balance and game. So he continues the practice, which he may not call a superstition. But what about the small toy lion that he carries with him on tour?

Like athletes in other team sports, bowlers also have routines for leaving their homes at exactly the same time and taking the exact route to the bowling lanes whenever they are in tournaments. Some pros get auto license plates that carry their initials plus the number 300—the perfect bowling score. Bowlers carry charms in their bowling bags, in a pocket, or around the neck. Yet, there are bowlers who refuse to carry certain good luck pieces. Senior tournament bowler John Hricsina told ESPN reporters that he never carries a dime in his pocket because he considers the coin bad luck.

During competition, some pros insist that they sit in specific places while waiting for their turns. A top bowling instructor and one-time pro Bill Bunetta not only sat in the same spot for each competition but also was very deliberate about the way he sat—his body posture was always the same. Others are very particular about their towels, even going so far as to make sure that a towel is folded in a precise manner after every use.

Dotty Fothergill, elected to the Women's International Bowling Congress Hall of Fame, would not bowl if her name was not spelled correctly on the scoresheet. Sometimes, she was listed as "Dot" or "Dorothy" or just the initial D. In such cases, she would refuse to compete until her name was written in as Dotty.

The right name is also important to Dale Glenn. From the beginning of his bowling career, he has preferred to be known by his nickname "Eagle," and in 1982 legally changed his name to Dale Eagle. He loves America's symbol and at the start of each session of a tournament, he lets loose with his impression of an eagle's screech. Perhaps this is his way of calling for the king of birds, which was once believed to be a bearer of power, vigor, and courage (particularly if you would drink its blood or eat it!).

Bingo and Other Indoor Games

Unlike bowling, many other indoor games are passive recreational activities. People need no particular physical skills to play and they truly depend on luck to win. Many of these games also involve gambling, which in itself is a superstitious practice. People who attend weekly bingo games pay for the bingo cards they use and if the letters and numbers on their cards are filled to spell out a "bingo," the cardholders expect to win cash or other prizes.

To be a winner, avid bingo players may insist on playing only at specific tables or places, buying a certain number of cards each time, or buying only cards with 7, 11, or 13 in a corner. Some wear lucky clothes. Others sit on special pillows with the word Bingo stitched or crocheted on top. If the game is not going well, players turn their pillows over, Bingo-side down.

Many place a lucky coin, religious medal, rabbit's foot, family photo, a small carved wooden figure, or some other favorite charm on the table above their cards. It's common for players to insist on a particular color for their plastic chips or ink daubers used to mark the bingo cards. When they win, players usually keep the cash separate from other spending money. "I never use my winnings to buy snacks or drinks," one woman says. "That's only for buying more bingo cards."

When it comes to card games, players depend on a lucky combination or deal of the cards to win. Before some players will deal, they kiss, blow on, or talk to the deck for luck. Touching a "good" card with an index finger before shuffling is supposed to assure a winning hand. Some players refuse to cut the cards before they are dealt because, as they say, "I don't want to cut my luck." Others say, "Cut them thin; you will win." Or they cut the cards toward themselves to bring luck their way.

Leo Sparkia always cuts cards in a special way that his friends call the "Holy Poke." When he's ready to deal, he sticks his finger on a spot alongside the deck, pushes a number of cards out and stacks that bunch on top. His fellow players swear that is usually a lucky cut.

Bad luck comes to those who drop a card on the floor, sing, hum, or whistle during a game. Other unlucky actions include crossing your legs, picking up the cards before the entire hand has been dealt, letting someone look over your shoulder, or lending someone money while you're in a game.

According to an old Italian proverb, "He who is lucky in love should never play cards." That superstition is still alive in many different countries today and is most often stated as "Lucky in cards, unlucky in love," or as the reverse: "Unlucky in cards, lucky in love."

Don't expect good fortune if you are dealt a four of clubs for your first hand. You aren't likely to win a hand if you hold a pair of aces and a pair of eights. The combination is called a deadman's hand. According to legend, a hero of the American West was playing cards and held two aces and two eights when he was shot dead by one of his enemies. Naturally, the hand became associated with a tragic end and now signifies a loss.

In gambling casinos, card tables are covered with felt to ward off a bad omen: playing on a bare table is bad luck. But it is possible to bring good fortune into a casino, as well. In some parts of Europe, hunchbacks have been hired to bring good luck to gamblers. Just touching a person with a curved spine was thought to be good luck, even though for many centuries people worldwide have feared those with physical deformities. Because little was known about the causes of deformed spines, dwarfed limbs, or other handicaps, people believed that physical disabilities stemmed from evil spirits or influences. Gamblers, however, believed just the reverse. They paid to touch a hunchbacked person for luck.

"Come Seven, Come Eleven"

Dice games are popular in most casinos, and many players who shoot dice talk to or blow or spit on the cubes to encourage a roll that will bring them cash winnings. Some people believe it's lucky to rub their dice on another person, particularly if that person happens to be a good friend. Crossing two fingers on one hand while shooting with the other is another way to bring luck with the dice. Snapping the fingers may prevent "snake eyes" or a pair of ones, the lowest possible number on the dice.

Numbers are of course the basis of dice shooting, and the number of dots that turn up when the cubes stop rolling determine what the player will win. Thus the saying "Come seven, come eleven" is a chant expected to produce a winning roll.

The dots on dice also foretell a person's future. If you roll a one, you are likely to get an important letter in the mail. Two dots signify a successful trip; three means you may be surprised by someone or some event. Nobody wants to roll a four—it's a sign of trouble. Five means some kind of change will take place in your family. When the number six turns up, you're in luck. Money, perhaps a large sum, is coming your way.

Pin Ball Banter

Although video games have replaced many of the once very popular "flipper games" in pinball machines, pinball enthusiasts still abound. For those who play the games, the challenge is to beat the machine, manipulating flippers in the machine to send five steel balls, one at a time, into pockets for a score. Most pinball players will use only those machines that "give you a fighting chance," as Jerome Boston, a college student and avid player, puts it. He notes that "a good machine should have lots of things on it—bumpers, tunnels, channels—things that challenge and give you something to do, but the machines shouldn't be placed on a slanted or uneven floor or left without repairs so that you can't possibly win."

To win, players resort to a number of magical practices. Talking to the steel ball is one. But a player does not want anyone else to talk to or about what the ball is doing in the game. "That is sure to put a hex on it," Jerome says. "See, if you start a really good game and it looks like you're going to win and someone mentions that fact, well, you'll lose. You might as well give up right then. That's the superstition. Not that I believe it exactly, but if you get too confident that you'll win, you'll lose your concentration and blow the game."

Pinball players also use a lot of body language to help them win. Sometimes it's a gentle tapping on the machine, but more often it's a great shaking, rattling, and rolling. Jerome explains it this way: "One of the best skills in the game is to save a ball that looks lost. You get it back with good flips and good shaking [of the machine]—not too much, but just enough so the machine doesn't tilt and you have to forfeit. Anyone who doesn't play that way isn't really playing. Like I say, the real thrill is in beating the machine," Jerome says. And that, as any pinball player would tell you, takes some luck, too.

Lotteries

In many parts of the United States, people play the lottery. This gambling game is big business in more than half the states, with annual sales in the billions of dollars. People buy cards or tickets with a series of numbers they have selected or a computer has selected for them, betting that those numbers will be drawn for cash winnings. Most hope for huge jackpots. But a very small percentage of those who play the lotteries actually win multi-million-dollar jackpots.

Nevertheless, people continue to play lotteries, using countless different methods for selecting numbers. They may believe that their birthdates are lucky, or they bet on their social security numbers, or the numbers of their street address, or the numbers on the jerseys worn by their favorite athletes.

In the Northwest, some lottery players may pick numbers that turn up when they use a device called a Six-Picker, created by a Richland, Washington, inventor in 1986. The device is actually a plastic cylinder that holds small numbered balls. To use the Six-

Picker, a person has to shake up the balls in the cylinder, then allow six balls to roll into an attached plastic pipe. The numbers that turn up in the pipe are the numbers to select for a lottery ticket.

Can a lottery player win with the Six-Picker? Nobody, including the inventor, will make that claim. The idea is to let the device do the picking, leaving the possibility of winning a jackpot in the hands of Fate, or luck, or chance, or whatever the guardian of gamblers may be.

$\star$ **8** $\star$

GONE FISHIN'—
FOR LUCK

Although few people gamble on sport fishing, the activity frequently is called a game of chance. There are so many unknowns in this recreational pursuit (as well as commercial fishing) that almost everyone who fishes has her or his own set of superstitions. Yet, there are some common beliefs surrounding the fishing sport and trade. Many who fish believe that "When the wind is from the east, the fish bite the least. When the wind is from the west, the fish bite the best." This is just one version of a rhyme that has been passed on from one generation to the next over many centuries:

When the wind is to the north,
The fisherman he goes not forth;
When the wind is to the east,
'Tis neither good for man nor beast,
When the wind is to the south,
It blows the bait in the fish's mouth;
When the wind is to the west,
Then 'tis at the very best.

Other long-standing fishing superstitions have to do with increasing one's catch:

If a barefoot woman passes you on the way to the wharf or launching place for your boat, take heed—the fish are not likely to bite. Your fishing also could suffer if you should happen to meet a pig on the way to your favorite fishing spot.

To make the fish bite, spit on your bait before casting it in the water.

Throw away the first catch for luck.

After the first catch, keep an unwanted fish until you've finished fishing. If you throw it back into the water right away, few fish will bite.

While fishing, don't change rods; it's bad luck.

It's unlucky to sit on an overturned bucket while you fish.

If anyone asks how many fish you've caught so far, don't answer or that will be the end of your catch for the day.

Fish Stories

Almost all of the superstitions just described would be refuted by some avid sports fisherman who believes just the opposite. A number of fishing enthusiasts say they take along their *lucky* buckets to sit on, and argue that changing poles is a way to lure fish and increase their catch. And "Never, never would I throw away the first catch," insisted the late Raymond McIntyre, a legendary fisherman in his South Bend, Indiana, neighborhood.

Most people who fish for sport personalize their superstitions. One woman had a cushion that she said brought her lucky catches. An elderly man says, "I never wash my hat; that takes all the luck out of it." He also showed off a set of lucky oars that had to be used on his fishing boat.

"When you break for lunch and fry fish, you better hope the pieces curl up because that means the fish will bite well that afternoon," a longtime fisherman says.

A number of fishermen in rural areas warned that "fish won't bite if the cows are lying down in the field."

Fishing beliefs and folklore are sometimes distinct to a region. "In the South where I first went fishing with my daddy, we didn't dare step over anyone else's pole. It was bad luck. I hear that yet today," says Leona Barnes who goes fishing "every chance I get" and has done so for more than forty years. "When I was a kid, we didn't talk while fishing—that was supposed to run the fish away," she says. "Catching a turtle would do the same thing. We used to catch these little turtles that had a bad smell, kill the things, and throw them back into the water. That was to get rid of the turtle hex. Another thing: you weren't supposed to take a pregnant woman fishing because that would bring the snakes out—bad luck for anybody!"

In Tarpon Springs, Florida, where sponge fishing is not only a recreation but also a highly successful trade among Greek fishermen, many believe it is unlucky to go out to sea on Tuesday. Greek sponge fishers also refuse to go to sea before Epiphany, a religious observance on January 6 each year.

Many European fishermen refuse to leave port on Friday and will wait until one minute into Saturday to set out. Apparently, the Friday taboo is related to the old English rhyme: "Sunday sail, never fail/Friday sail, ill luck and gale." But Scottish fishermen may be an exception, since it is their rule never to sail on Sunday.

If the captain of an English fishing boat brings friends on board, the fish had better bite that day. Otherwise, the crew will take the ship back to shore and ask the guests to leave, politely of course.

Scottish fishermen once dreaded hearing anyone call their name or cross their path after they'd left home for their boat. These were considered sure signs of misfortune. So to X-out the evil, the fisherman had to pull out a knife, draw a cross on the ground, spit on it, then say a few magical words.

Fishermen in the British Isles have long believed that pigs on board a fishing vessel will bring bad luck. Rabbits and ministers and anyone else who might be different from the crew are in the same category.

On the other hand, American fishermen have taken animal companions aboard their vessels. Monkeys have been common mascots at sea.

In Norwegian communities (both in Norway or those that have been established by émigrés to the United States), fishing folk frown on wearing white while fishing. Even a white fishing pole should be stashed because the fish won't bite if you use one.

In France, some fishermen not only follow the practice of throwing back the first catch but also fill the fish with wine, in the hope that other fish will want to imbibe.

West Indian fishermen wear various charms on necklaces and carry fragrant oils to ward off evil spirits who are attracted by unpleasant odors. Thus, the captain of a fishing ship also must throw his dirty shirt over the ship's leeward side—the side sheltered from the wind.

Fishermen along the coast of Ireland say they can predict fair or foul weather for fishing. According to folklorist Horace Beck, there is a coastal cliff covered with chalky deposits that appears to change with weather conditions. The deposits make the cliff appear to be a ship under sail. When the "ship" seems headed for shore, the fishermen expect a storm and stay home. If the ship appears to be going out to sea, so can the fishermen.

In some parts of the world, fishermen still paint eyes on the forward part of their ship's hull—"the better to see with, my dear," and thus protect the crew. Or holes might be bored into the rudders to let out evil spirits lurking around.

Of Ships and Boats

Many vessels also are surrounded by special superstitions of their own. The ritual of launching a ship is familiar. Usually someone smashes a bottle of champagne or other type of wine across the bow of a ship to christen it. According to Willard A. Heaps, who collected tales of various superstitious practices in all walks of life, the launching ceremony probably stems from an ancient Viking practice. It was common for Viking sailors to spread animal blood across the ship's prow to give it life and to protect the crew.

Most commercial fishermen and many who fish for sport would not go aboard an unchristened vessel. One story is told about a fisherman along the eastern U.S. seaboard, who launched a "dry" fishing boat in the late 1800s. His boat ran aground twice during the year, and the rudder completely broke off. So the fisherman pulled his boat ashore for repairs and then launched it again with a great crashing and splashing of a bottle of bubbly wine. Needless to say, the boat stayed afloat!

Many sailors and recreational boaters also carry lucky charms. These might be religious medals with the likeness of St. Christopher or St. Elmo, the protector of the seas. At one time, heart-shaped objects—particularly pin cushions shaped like hearts—were thought to bring good luck. Silver coins, white stones with holes in them, bones from horseshoe crabs, chestnuts, light-colored Brazilian nuts, seashells, pieces of coal, and black-handled knives are among other talismans that have been credited with protecting health, guarding against evil, and diluting the effects of bad omens at sea.

Earrings have been common charms and usually a seaman has worn only one. The practice was tied to an old belief that piercing an ear would help a sailor better see out of the opposite eye—the eye used for peering through the "spyglass" or telescope.

Sailors and boaters also have followed certain rules that have been steeped in superstition and have carried over to today's recreational boater:

Never whistle aboard a vessel because that's "whistling for the wind" and a dangerous gale could quickly appear.

If you buy a sailboat, you should secure a lucky coin at the bottom of the mast.

Don't paint a boat the color blue. (Some say stay away from green.)

If rats leave a ship before it goes to sea, beware.

Tragedy could strike. You've no doubt heard or read the saying: "Rats always desert a sinking ship."

You can take a black cat aboard a ship since, contrary to its bad luck rap, the black cat is a charm at sea. So is a cricket. Bring it aboard to change a string of unlucky events.

Don't carry a black suitcase or an umbrella aboard. If you ever find either of these unlucky items on a ship, you should toss it into the water to prevent misfortune.

Folklorist Horace Beck wrote about the bad luck associated with an umbrella his wife insisted on taking aboard a boat in Copenhagen during the summer of 1966. As he explains in his book *Folklore and the Sea*, he took the umbrella off the boat, but his wife brought it back aboard. As a result:

> *For the entire summer we had gales, fog, engine trouble, headwinds and sickness aboard. . . we ran aground in the English Channel. The weather began to deteriorate and the prospects looked very bleak. The ship lay over and the umbrella tumbled out. I stuck it in the sand alongside. The tide rose, the vessel floated, the wind moderated, and the rest of that summer and all the next were trouble-free.*

★ 9 ★

ANTICS
OF THE FANS

Want to help your ballteam win a game? Love to boost the chances for your favorite racer, boxer, golfer, bowler, or tennis player to be tops in her or his sport? If so, you may be one of millions of fans worldwide who try to influence the outcome of a competition with some form of "magic."

Not that all sports fans are superstitious. It's just that many people would like their favorite team or star athlete to have an "edge." How do they try to make that happen? Many fans wear hats, shirts, and jackets with their teams' logos and colors. Some send coins, medals, and other charms to their favorite sports stars. During the 1940s, the renowned Yankees slugger Joe DiMaggio was in a great hitting streak, and fans sent him all types of lucky charms so that he could keep the streak going.

Mass Fanfare

Mass fan support is another way to bring a team luck. Any baseball fan knows you have to stand up for the seventh inning stretch. How did such a practice get started? In earlier days, ballpark benches were so uncomfortable, spectators had to stand just to limber up and prevent cramps in their backs and legs. But why not stand up for the fifth inning—just beyond the halfway mark in the game? You've probably guessed: the number seven has long been considered lucky. Hence the seventh inning stretch.

Individual baseball teams also prompt massive fan displays. One year Milwaukee Brewers fans created three-cornered Styrofoam hats that looked like wedges of cheese (Wisconsin is known for its dairy products), and called themselves "cheese heads" as a way of boosting their team.

New York Yankees fans used to chant for one of their favorite hitters just before he came up to the plate. The sound of "Reg-gie! Reg-gie!" rolling in waves across the stands was a ritual calling not only on Reggie Jackson but also the gods of home runs.

Chicago Cubs baseball fans who always sit in the bleachers would not think of going into the stands or buying box seats. They are proud to be called "bleacher bums" and for several seasons made their presence known by wearing yellow hard hats for each game. They feel they bring their team luck. Cubs outfielder Gary Matthews agreed, and in 1984 had hats and T-shirts made for the left-field bleacher bums. Matthews believed the left-field crew created their own kind of magic for that season since the Cubs won the National League Eastern Division championship, although they were unable to make it to the world series.

The Cubs have not played in a world series for decades and that may be partly due to the Billy Goat curse. It seems that in the 1940s, a fan who owned a tavern called The Billy Goat in downtown Chicago always took a live goat, which he considered a kind of mascot for the Cubs, to Wrigley Field. But in 1945 when the Cubs did play in the world series, the goat was barred from the field. "Curse you all!" the tavern owner told team officials. "The Cubs will never be in another world series." So far they haven't, and the curse still holds, although fans have plenty of ideas, which they'll loudly expound upon, on how it could be wiped out.

The Boston Red Sox seem to be under a curse as well. The owner of the team in 1918 was Harry Frezee. In order to raise money for a show called "No No Nanette" Frezee sold Babe Ruth to the Yankees for $100,000. The Sox have not won a world series since then.

Massive public support is common for basketball and football teams—both professional and amateur. When the Middletown, Ohio, high school basketball team was winning so many games in the 1950s, home-town fans developed a passion for purple, which they considered a lucky color. Purple clothing became the fashion. Purple pants. Purple sweaters. Purple jackets. Purple hats. Purple ribbons. Purple shoes. Purple socks. Even one of the players took up the purple passion, carrying purple sweatbands whenever he went on road trips.

In another Ohio town, it was the football fans who dressed for luck. Most residents of Masillon, Ohio, are boosters of the Tigers, their high school team. Calling their community Tigertown, Masillon folks say, "Any-one who doesn't support the team doesn't belong in this town." To dramatize their togetherness, Tiger fans wear orange and black for their football heroes. Many are apt to sprout orange wigs and orange and black striped tiger faces when the team is playing.

Fans of professional teams are no less enthusiastic. When the Chicago Bulls put on their charmed black shoes for their spectacular 1989 season, the fans got into the act, too. There was a run on black sneakers in the shoe stores. And the red bull mascot added black shoes to his costume as did the cheerleaders.

On Ice

Hockey fans often go way out to bring victory to their teams. Fans of the Calgary Flames, for example, painted their faces in bright orange and red flame designs to help their team win the 1989 Stanley Cup. During seasons when the Detroit Red Wings made it to the playoffs for the Stanley Cup, fans threw octopuses on the ice before a game. The strange ritual began with a fan who thought an octopus with its eight tentacles would help the Red Wings win the two series, or a total of eight games, for the 1952 Stanley Cup competition. Apparently, the eight-limbed creature had its desired effect. The Red Wings won, and for nearly forty years fans have kept the superstition—although certainly not the original octopus—alive.

Chicago Blackhawks fans take part in a routine that started during the 1982 season when the Blackhawks won forty-seven games. Some believe the ritual is disrespectful. From the time the organist begins to play the "Star Spangled Banner," fans scream so loudly that no one can hear the music. As a *Chicago Sun-Times* reporter noted, Blackhawks fans are part of a "hardcore hockey cult," and while they cheer madly as the anthem is being played, a huge American flag is being unfurled from the top balcony. The gesture shows their patriotism, many fans say.

After the organ stops playing, two fans who are brothers begin a march to some steel girders in the stadium where they pound in a rhythm that is supposed to represent the sound of Native American drums. Another Blackhawks fan, who wears an elaborate Indian headdress, lights sparklers to brighten the outlook for Chicago's hockey team.

Another rather bizarre happening has taken place at the Los Angeles Kings arena. There an avid hockey fan and radio personality, now called "Lucky Butt," comes down before a game and sits his bare behind on the ice. In 1989 during playoff games with the Edmonton Oilers, "Lucky Butt" did not show up for his bare bottom ritual. As a result, he was blamed for the Kings' loss.

Racing Luck to the Finish

Since it became a custom centuries ago to wager or bet on the outcome of horse races, racing fans consistently have used magic practices to try to bring a favorite horse across the finish line. Even though most bettors study the track records of horses to determine a winner, they also depend on lucky hunches, charms, and encounters with people and things that might bring them good fortune.

One custom of more than a century ago was to grind up the bones of a toad or frog and scatter the powder over a horse, thus giving the animal more power. Some race fans carried a frog's bone for luck.

Another practice originated in England where many racing fans would refuse to bet on a horse until after they had seen or touched a chimney sweep. At one time chimney sweeping was a common occupation. Sweeps were needed to clean flues that became clogged with soot and were fire hazards. According to an old English legend, the idea that luck appeared with a sweep came about because a sooty sweep happened to save a monarch's life by stopping the king's runaway horse. Even today a sweep may be invited on occasion to bring luck to a wedding, as well as a horse race.

Early in the twentieth century, European racegoers would not bet on a horse whose name began with W. The reason? It seems that a Gypsy had predicted a horse named Blue Gown would win the Epson Derby, but she mistakenly wrote down the name *Blew Gown*. The horse's owner pointed out the misspelling, saying that there was no *w* in the horse's name. This infuriated the Gypsy, who did not like appearing foolish in public. So she declared that during her lifetime any horse with a name that began with W would lose in the Epson Derby.

The Gypsy's curse held until after her death. Then

her relatives decided it was time to bet large sums on a horse called Windsor Lad running in the Epson Derby that year. Indeed the Lad was free of the curse, winning the Derby, and paying the Gypsy relatives 7 to 1 on their bets.

The Ultimate Fans: Family People

In many sports, close relatives of athletes and coaches can be lucky influences. Wives or husbands of athletes frequently sit in their own special places to cast their good luck glances toward spouses competing

in games. The wife of basketball coach Stan Albeck sat in her particular spot during each game; if Albeck couldn't see her, he felt bad luck was brewing.

Amateur boxers who have trained with their fathers feel it is bad luck to get into the ring for a bout without the "old man in my corner." Family photos often accompany boxers—and many other athletes—to assure good fortune.

The mother of an LPGA golfer wears a special dress and perfume when her daughter is competing in a tournament.

Seattle Mariners Ken Griffey, Jr., feels the baseball gods are with him when his mom is in the stands.

Across the sea, another mother brought a bit of magic to Japanese baseball star Sadaharu Oh who was about to play a crucial game in 1977. He had the chance to break the record for home runs, then held by U.S. slugger Hank Aaron. Oh's mother brought a small box of crickets to the locker room. The crickets were a gift for Oh's daughters who, the grandmother thought, would enjoy hearing "voices" from the country. In his autobiography, Oh said he held the box of crickets up to his ear and listened to their sounds. "When I left my locker and headed for the field, I had no feeling of tiredness. I could feel in my bones that this indeed was the night. . . . The quietness my mother had brought surrounded me like a spell. . . ." By the third inning, it "indeed was the night." Oh hit the record-breaking home run—his 756th.

★ 10 ★

WHY SUPERSTITIONS
IN SPORTS AND GAMES?

Anyone who excels in a physical sport knows that it is necessary to practice, train, be well-conditioned physically, and learn as much as possible about winning techniques. Seldom, though, do athletes get to the top all by themselves. They receive help not only from coaches, trainers, and medical experts, but also from sports psychologists and computer technicians.

With computer software, a professional baseball coach or manager can advise a slugger like Darryl Strawberry what to expect when he's up against a pitcher such as Orel Hershiser. Electronic programs also have been devised to keep track of professional football players' injuries and treatment and thus provide instant backup for any future medical aid. Other computer software assists pit crews at race tracks, providing information on how to fine tune engines and what aerodynamic adjustments are necessary on a race car.

But in spite of all the new technology and expert advice, many professional athletes (and amateurs, too) still take part in "magical" practices. Why? One reason may be that in many cases athletes are evenly matched in physical and mental abilities, training, and conditioning. So to win, athletes may feel they need a "lucky break," some chance happening that provides an advantage.

There's another more basic reason that sports magic survives. Over the ages, people have held on to beliefs in the magical properties of charms and rituals in order to have some control over their destinies and to deal with the unknown. In sports, there are plenty of unknowns, and superstitious practices may be one of the few constant factors. As one coach explains: "There is so little certainty in competitive situations—very little we can really control—so why not wear dirty socks or a favorite sweatband or listen to the same music before each competition? It's reassuring."

Some superstitions do relieve anxiety and can have a calming effect. By following the same pattern, ritual, or routine before every competition, athletes can sometimes create the mental and physical harmony they need to win. On the other hand, if they worry about all the possible unknowns, athletes may be unable to do their best.

Clinical psychologist Dorcas Susan Butt, a former Canadian tennis star, notes in her book *The Psychol-*

ogy of Sport, how a basketball player or archer could improve performance with a bit of ritual:

> *If a basketball player is having difficulty on free throws or an archer is releasing shots too soon, then it is possible to train the individual to associate a "key word" with the moment of release of ball or arrow. The basketball player may think . . . or say aloud "sink." This trick may help the athlete focus on the task and control unwanted anxiety or distraction at crucial moments.*

However, sports psychologists, coaches, and athletes themselves caution that no one should depend on external tricks alone, particularly when it involves rituals. Some are so complex that they may be impossible to follow each time a competition comes up. Suppose you forget the particular order of a ritual and become distracted when unsure of what to do next for luck? Or maybe you follow all of your superstitious practices to the letter but still lose in competition.

A good luck charm can create problems also. Maybe the charm is misplaced or lost. Then what? Anyone who depends on a good luck piece to do well in sports is really making excuses for lack of training or preparation, say many athletes.

The point is, superstition is harmful when it becomes more important than developing self-confidence and improving skills. One skill helpful in virtually every sport is mental imagery, psychologists say.

Many books and magazine articles have been written explaining how to practice imagery to mentally prepare for a sport. Imagery is especially helpful in developing strategy for team sports such as football and in games such as golf that require concentration. As Tom Jewell, tournament director for the JC Penny Classic, explains: "Some professional golfers may carry good luck charms, but they still use the 'image' method to prepare for a shot; they 'image' what the swing will look like, where the shot will go, and so on. A golfer addresses the ball in a certain way, swings at a certain angle and speed. Each golfer prepares for a shot in the same way each time."

Well-known golf champ Jack Nicklaus once put it this way: "I never hit a shot, even in practice, without having a very sharp, in-focus picture of it in my head."

Positive self-talk also helps any contender get ready for competition. If you tell yourself you are lousy or no good or make similar negative self-assessments, you could be setting yourself up for failure. A ball-player who appears to be mumbling or speaking magical words over a ball may instead be using self-talk to make a successful pitch, or free throw. Muhammad Ali's "I'm the greatest!" was not just an idle boast. It was part of his routine to mentally prepare for competition. In short, if you are going to compete in sports, games, or life itself, you need to have faith in your own abilities.

But there's still that element called luck. How do you deal with good or bad luck in competition? Do any superstitious practices really work, bring the desired effect? People who accept only scientific evidence and logical reasoning might say "no way!" Yet some of those same folks may still engage in superstitious practices.

So what's the bottom-line advice? Experts on human behavior suggest that if you've done all you possibly can to prepare physically and mentally for a competition, then a convenient superstition won't hurt you. If it makes you feel comfortable to knock on wood, rub that medal, step over a line, spit with the wind, cross your fingers but not the bats or hockey sticks or fishing poles, or to avoid the color green and the number 13, then get on with it. Perhaps you'll be victorious in whatever you do. Here's wishing you "Good Luck!"

FOR FURTHER READING

ABC Sports. *The Complete Book of Sports Facts*. Princeton, NJ: American Broadcasting Company Merchandising, Inc. and Norback & Company, Inc., 1981.

Ashley, Leonard R. N. *The Wonderful World of Superstition, Prophecy and Luck*. New York: Dembner Books, 1984.

Beck, Horace. *Folklore and the Sea* (Chapter XI). Middletown, Connecticut: Wesleyan University Press, 1973.

Becker, Judy. "Superstition in Sport." *International Journal of Sport Psychology*, December 1975, pp. 148–152.

Bodo, Peter. "Tennis Superstitions: The Surprising Fetishes of the Pros." *Tennis*, April 1977, pp. 62–70; 72.

Bonnerjea, Biren. *A Dictionary of Superstitions and Mythology*. Detroit: Singing Tree Press, 1969; London: Folk Press Ltd., 1927.

Bortstein, Larry. "Superstition." *Golf Journal*, January/February 1977, pp. 83–85.

Butt, Dorcas Susan. *The Psychology of Sport*. New York: Van Nostrand Reinhold Company, Inc., 1987.

Chance, Paul. "Knock on Wood." *Psychology Today*, October 1988, pp. 68–69.

Chaundler, Christine. *Every Man's Book of Superstitions*. New York: Philosophical Library, 1970.

Coffin, T. C., ed. *Our Living Traditions*. New York: Basic Books, 1968.

Diaz, Jaime. "New Latin Twist on the Pro Tour." *Sports Illustrated*, April 7, 1986, pp. 87–91.

Dutton, R.A.M. "Some Sporting Superstitions." *Parks and Recreation* (London), May 1982, p. 41.

Einstein, Charles, ed. *The Fireside Book of Baseball* (4th Ed.). New York: Simon & Schuster, 1987.

Ferm, Vergiluis. *A Brief Dictionary of American Superstitions*. New York: Philisophical Library, 1959.

Frayne, Trent. "Mind Over What Really Matters." *Macleans*, May 23, 1983, p. 46.

Garfinkel, Charlie. "Superstitions of the Players." *National Racquetball*, September 1982, pp. 9–11.

Gipe, George. *The Great American Sports Book*. New York: Doubleday, 1978.

Goldstein, Steve. "Superstitious? Naah!" *World Tennis*, February 1985, pp. 36–39.

Griffith, Linda Lewis. "You're Not—Knock on Wood—Superstitious?" *Women's Sports*, October 1981, p. 47.

Gunther, Max. *The Luck Factor*. New York: Macmillan, 1977.

Hale, Christina, ed. *The Encyclopedia of Superstitions*. London: Hutchinson of London, 1961.

Hall, George. "Mind Over Matter." *Goal*, May/June 1985, pp. 26–28.

Heaps, Willard A. *Superstition!* (Chapter 10) Nashville, Camden, New York: Thomas Nelson, Inc., 1972.

Hersch, Hank. "The Good Wood." *Sports Illustrated*, April 14, 1986, pp. 68–80.

Horn, Jack. "The Superstitious Athlete: Controlling Uncertainty." *Psychology Today*, September 1976, p. 30.

Jahoda, Gustav. *The Psychology of Superstition*. London and Baltimore, MD: The Penguin Press, 1969.

Kay, Linda. "A Little Bit of Voodoo." *Women's Sports and Fitness*, June 1986, pp. 26–27.

Kleinmann, Leanne. "Old-Shoe Superstitions." *American Health*, June 1988, p. 82.

Ladouceur, Albert. "Beware the Black Cat!" *Sport Selection Magazine*, January 1979, pp. 20–21; 78.

Lasne, Sophie and Gaultier, André Pascal. *A Dictionary of Superstitions*. Englewood Cliffs, NJ: Prentice-Hall, 1984.

Lessiter, Mike. *The Names of the Games*. Chicago: Contemporary Books, 1988.

Maple, Eric. *Superstition and the Superstitious*. New York: A. S. Barnes & Co., 1971.

McCallum, Jack. "By the Numbers." *Sports Illustrated*, February 24, 1986, pp. 62–72.

Nash, Bruce, and Allan Zullo. *Baseball Confidential*™. New York, London, Toronto, Sydney, Tokyo: Pocket Books, 1988.

Perl, Lila. *Blue Monday and Friday the Thirteenth*. New York: Clarion Books, 1986.

Planer, F. E. *Superstition*. London: Cassel Ltd., 1980.

Pope, Edwin. "Me, Superstitious?" *Golf Digest*, May 1978, pp. 180–182.

Schwartz, Alvin (collector). *Cross Your Fingers, Spit in Your Hat: Superstitions and Other Beliefs*. New York: Lippincott, 1974.

Seymour, Harold. *Baseball: The Golden Age*. Oxford: Oxford University Press, 1971.

"Spooked in the Cradle of the Deep." *Changing Times*, June 1970, p. 24.

Sullivan, Constance, ed. *Spirit of Sport*. Boston: Little, Brown and Company/Polaroid Corporation, 1985.

Sullivan, George. *Sports Superstitions*. New York: Coward, McCann, 1978.

"Superstition." *Sports Illustrated*, February 8, 1988, pp. 86–94.

Thompson, C. J. S. *The Hand of Destiny Folklore and Superstition for Everyday Life*. New York: Bell Publishing Company, 1989.

Trogdon, Wendell. *Basket Cases*. Evanston, IL: The Highlander Press, 1989.

Wieder, Bob. "Superstitions and Other Baseball Essentials." *A's News*, September 27, 1982, pp. 10–13.

Womack, Mari. "Sports Magic." *Human Behavior*, September 1978, pp. 43–44.

Yagoda, Ben. "Getting Psyched." *Esquire*, April 1982, pp. 31; 34.

Zimmer, Judith. "Courting the Gods of Sport." *Psychology Today*, July 1984, pp. 36–39.